STANDING ON BOTH FEET

Standing on Both Feet

Voices of Older Mixed Race Americans

Cathy J. Tashiro

Paradigm Publishers
Boulder • London

Published in the United States by Paradigm Publishers, 5589 Arapahoe Avenue, Boulder, CO 80303 USA.

Paradigm Publishers is the trade name of Birkenkamp & Company, LLC, Dean Birkenkamp, president and publisher.

Library of Congress Cataloging-in-Publication Data

Tashiro, Cathy J.
  Standing on both feet : voices of older mixed race Americans / by Cathy Tashiro.
    p. cm.
  Includes bibliographical references and index.
  ISBN 978-1-59451-983-3 (pbk : alk. paper)
  1. Racially mixed people—United States—Social conditions. 2. Racially mixed people—Race identity—United States. 3. Racially mixed people—United States—Attitudes. 4. Older people—United States—Social conditions. 5. Older people—United States—Attitudes. 6. Miscegenation—Social aspects—United States 7. Race—Social aspects—United States.
  I. Title.
  E184.A1T37 2012
  305.800973—dc23

                                                                                    2011024630

Printed and bound in the United States of America on acid-free paper that meets the standards of the American National Standard for Permanence of Paper for Printed Library Materials.

Designed and Typeset in Adobe Garamond by Straight Creek Bookmakers.

16 15 14 13

Contents

Preface

Like the people in this book, I am an older mixed race American. I was born in Cincinnati in 1946 to a Nisei (second generation, U.S. born) Japanese American father who became a doctor; my mother is from a white working-class family in Kentucky. My parents got together right at the end of World War II, when there was a lot of anti-Japanese sentiment, and my white grandfather initially disowned my mother for marrying my father. Eventually, when the children started coming, my mother was accepted back into her family.

My early years were spent in some very remote places in upstate New York and Michigan. My father had a series of jobs working in tuberculosis sanitariums, and we lived on the grounds of these institutions. It only occurred to me much later that these might have been the only jobs available to him as a Japanese American doctor in the immediate post–World War II era. We were very isolated, and my happiest childhood memories are of the summers we spent at my Japanese grandparents' summer home, because my aunt and uncle and their mixed race children were also there. It felt like we were our own tribe, and this was the only time in my childhood when I remember having a sense of belonging. It never occurred to me that my sense of alienation was related to race, but I had a vague sense of how skin color and ancestry set us apart.

When asked, I usually told people I was half Japanese, but when we visited my grandparents on my father's side in the summer, I knew I wasn't Japanese. They ate weird food and spoke Japanese, which I didn't. My father tried his very best to be a super American. Assimilation was the goal for Japanese Americans his age in this postwar period. He taught us no Japanese, and he expected my mother to cook American food. I remember wanting to be more Japanese, or perhaps thinking I should be. One brief endeavor at becoming Japanese was my attempt to kneel for long periods on the rubber cushions taken from the couch at my Japanese grandparents' house. I'm not sure where I got this idea, maybe from the movie *Sayonara*. I knew Grandma thought this was ridiculous. She certainly didn't spend her time kneeling in a kimono. She usually wore an old housedress while taking on projects like darning socks or painting the house—and memorably berating my grandfather in Japanese. Kneeling was painful and quickly forgone. Somehow I learned a few important basic words, like *mizu* (water) and *gohan* (rice). I think that in a very basic way, I was searching for who I was or where I fit. My images of what being Japanese might be were of the same distorted caricatures shared by the general population. The contradictions abounded; I remember the old World War II paperbacks at my Japanese grandparents' home depicting ugly, buck-toothed Japanese war pilots as the enemy. When we got a television in the early 1950s, one of my father's favorite shows was *Victory at Sea,* a documentary of World War II naval battles, primarily carried out against the Japanese.

I spent my formative adolescent years in the late 1950s and early 1960s in an upstate New York town so small it could barely be called a town; no other people of color or mixed race lived there. Although white, the town was ethnically diverse. There was "Guinea Alley" (this was before the advent of politically correct speech), where many of the Italians lived, and being Catholic seemed to forge a bond that overcame ethnic boundaries for Italians and Poles. I didn't think of my town as white. To my adolescent eyes, people just were who they were. But who I was and how I fit in were mysteries. "Race" at that time and place meant "Negro." I wasn't Negro, but I knew I was different.

I will never forget the first time I saw the public face of someone who looked like me, when I went to see the film *South Pacific,* which was released in 1958 and played at my small-town movie theater. The part of Liat was played by France Nguyen, who was born to a Vietnamese mother and French father in France. She was supposed to be Polynesian. The ethnicity of her character's mother, Bloody Mary, the Chinese Hawaiian souvenir dealer, didn't match that of the woman playing her either, Juanita Hall, the great actress and singer of obviously mixed African American ancestry. Like the public, Hollywood has long had difficulty "placing" people of mixed race, which is interesting given that *South Pacific* is about prejudice against intermarriage and having mixed race children. But that night, I wasn't thinking about any of that. I was astonished that someone who was clearly (to me) neither wholly "Oriental" nor wholly "Caucasian" was on the screen, someone who looked like me. I remember going to the corner store after the movie, buying something, and lifting my face to the Italian owner with a feeling of pride, a sense that I was somehow placed and recognizable for the first time in my life. I was so excited, I couldn't sleep that night.

Flash forward to 1990. The words "People of Mixed Blood" leapt off the page at me. I was leafing through a booklet of classes to distract myself while at work in the student health center at the University of California, Berkeley. Illustrated by a picture of a professor and students of racially ambiguous appearance, the title advertised a class taught by Terry Wilson of the Native American Studies Department, the first class ever offered on the topic of mixed race at an academic institution. I was astounded and thrilled that someone had named what I struggled to understand, even in middle age, and that it was considered legitimate enough to merit a class at Berkeley. The phrases "mixed blood" and, later, "mixed race" brought clarity to my own previously inchoate experience. Naming mixed race made it real and worthy of examination. That moment marked a major change in consciousness for me.

I arranged to audit that class and immediately found myself surrounded by students at least twenty years my junior. Many assumed the right to identify as they pleased. Most had been born after the civil rights movement, and their awareness of conditions in America prior to their births was pretty sketchy. To me, as an older person of mixed race, they radiated naiveté and an enviable aura of freedom and optimism. They took so much for granted that people of my generation and older couldn't when we were their age. Taking this class marked the beginning of a new direction in my life, culminating in my enrollment in a doctoral program in sociology and my decision to do my research on older people of mixed race.

I've told a bit of my story because it includes elements that appeared again and again in the stories of the people of mixed race of a certain age in this book. Like them, I experienced a dissonance between parts of my background. My sense of possibilities for identity was sometimes transformed in a moment, sometimes over periods of political evolution, both the country's and my own. Perhaps most importantly, mixed race people my age and older did not see ourselves reflected in the world around us. Whereas today younger people of mixed race have the chance to see others who look like them in the media, sports world, and public life, when the people in this book were young, few minorities were publicly visible—and certainly not people of acknowledged mixed race, which often carried a taint of shame when it was addressed at all. Without such a reflection, a coherent sense of self-recognition was hard-won for many of us. The notion of "standing on both feet" was a distant dream. The very terms we used and how race was defined were different.

I collected the stories of the people in this book between 1996 and 1998. Since then, there has been a sea change in the country's awareness of people of mixed race. In 2000, for the first time in the history of the U.S. census, respondents were allowed to self-identify with more than one racial group. A mixed race son of an immigrant was elected president of the United States in 2008. Such events were unimaginable when the people in this book were growing up. In the academy, we now have mixed race studies and a blossoming of well-conducted research on people of mixed race. However, the vast majority of published work on people of mixed race remains concerned with adolescents and young adults, which effaces the degree to which historical context shapes identity. Since I collected these stories, some of the people I interviewed have passed away. Yet, it is more important than ever that their stories be heard, because they form a living link to a past that still shadows the present. This book is dedicated to them with overwhelming gratitude for their great generosity and the profound insights they shared with me. It is written for all people of mixed race in hopes that each of you will find something of yourself within its covers.

Acknowledgments

This work could not have been done without the support and encouragement of many individuals. I was well supported by the Department of Social and Behavioral Sciences of the University of California, San Francisco, in conducting the original research upon which this book is based. In particular, Gay Becker brought dedication, knowledge, and critical insight to bear on my writing. She was consistently supportive of my work and gave me the confidence to find my own voice. No one could ask for more from a mentor, and she is deeply missed by the multitude of individuals whose lives she touched. The University of Washington has also been supportive of my research on people of mixed race. Thanks also to Francesca Rivera, who designed the graphic charts in this book.

Special thanks to the former members of the Multiracial Alternatives Project of the University of California, Berkeley. The MAP group, as it came to be known, comprised graduate students doing work on some aspect of mixed race when I was in graduate school. Being a part of this group of fabulous mixed race women was transformative for me. In particular, I want to acknowledge Kim DaCosta, Kaaryn Gustafson, Becky King O'Rian, Cindy Nakashima, Caroline Streeter, and Kendra Wallace. Each of them is an outstanding scholar in her own right, and all have advanced the state of mixed race scholarship tremendously.

My heartfelt gratitude goes out to the people who participated in this research. They were most generous to me with their time and vulnerability. Their stories enthralled me and demanded to be told. The words they chose spoke eloquently of the particular pains and dilemmas of older people of mixed race. My interactions with them were often profoundly moving. In addition to learning about them, I found something out about myself with each interview. This has been a dialectical process of discovery and self-discovery.

Finally, big thanks to my husband, Carl Anderson, whose patience has been surely tested through the long process of bringing this work to print. His love and support have been critical to any successes I may have achieved.

Introduction

> All of a sudden, I realized I was standing on two feet and that
> I had been hopping around on one foot, back and forth, all
> my life, and didn't know it. I didn't know I was hopping until
> I got both feet on the ground at the same time. I said, "Damn,
> this feels kind of good. It has to do with how secure can you be
> on one foot? It's very difficult to be secure, keep your balance.
> When I've got both feet on the ground, I can feel secure, I can
> feel grounded, I am grounded."
>
> —*Fred Johnson,*[1] *a mixed African American man,*
> *born in 1941, speaking of his discovery of the possibility of*
> *a mixed race identity*

When Fred Johnson was growing up and becoming a man, "standing on both feet" was not an option for people of mixed African American and white ancestry. Growing up in the Pacific Northwest in the 1940s and 1950s, despite the fact that his mother was white and his father was of mixed African American and Native American ancestry, Fred was a Negro according to the conventions of the time. He remembers his being the first "colored" family to move into a public housing project originally built to accommodate wartime defense workers. He describes the hostility he encountered from white children when he tried to explain his mixed ancestry. As a result, for much of his early life, he avoided the issue of race if at all possible. Fred has traveled a lot and first got interested in mixed race issues in the early 1980s when he joined a mixed race support group in the San Francisco Bay Area.

Todd Sasaki, a native Californian of similar age to Fred but of Japanese and Jewish ancestry, states that he didn't see himself as either

1

but indentifies himself as Eurasian if asked to do so on forms. Unlike Fred, Todd has few memories of being made aware of his nonwhite ancestry when he was growing up or of being made to define himself solely as Japanese—with one glaring exception. When he was three years old, he was sent to an internment camp because of his Japanese ancestry. His white mother chose to be interned with him, though she had the option of remaining free. In this case, something akin to the "one-drop rule" (Davis 1991), which has been applied to people of African ancestry in the United States like Mr. Johnson, was applied to people of Japanese ancestry. Individuals with as little as one-sixteenth Japanese "blood" could be imprisoned. In Todd's case, he and his mother were eventually able to leave the camp, but only under the condition that his mother "make a monthly report to the commander in chief of the military district that I had not committed any acts of sabotage," Todd told me.

Today, the equation of the presence of Japanese "blood" with a propensity to commit sabotage on the part of a three-year-old seems ridiculous, and the nation has officially repudiated the treatment of people of Japanese ancestry during World War II. An additional irony to Todd's story is that his mother, non-Japanese and white by U.S. definitions, at that very historical moment would have been subjected to the same ideology of race as "something in the blood," with life-or-death consequences, for being Jewish had she been living in Europe.

Fluctuations in official definitions of race have had direct personal meaning for people like Fred and Todd, as well as for Todd's "white" mother. Their stories indicate the contradictory, capricious, and politicized nature of race and racism. Both men discuss past times when they were identified by others and self-identified differently than they do in the present. Fred was a Negro in his youth growing up in Seattle. No other option was available to him at that time, although he was "standing on one foot." He discovered the possibility of a multiracial identity later in life when the growing population of young multiracials began to force mixed race into public discussion. Todd expresses a more episodic sense of identity than Fred. His appearance is racially ambiguous, and he is not easily recognized as a person of Asian ancestry. However, during World War II, he became essentially Japanese in the eyes of government authorities. Paradoxically, he also remembers feeling utterly Jewish and ready to enlist in the Israeli army when the Six Day War started in 1968.

This book explores the contradictions and conundrums of identity for Fred, Todd, and eighteen other older people of mixed African American/white and mixed Asian American/white ancestry, born between 1902 and 1951 and living in the San Francisco Bay Area, as they talk about the significance of race in their lives, past and present. Both Fred and Todd have lived through dramatic changes in racial policies and politics. However, the memory of those times keeps them present, embodied by the persons who lived through them.

Study Population

I chose people from mixed African American/white and mixed Asian American/white backgrounds for a couple of reasons. First, I sought people who were mixed between what I call a "subordinate" group (meaning from a group considered to be nonwhite) and the "dominant" (or white) group (Tashiro 2002). Historically in the United States, the racial boundary of most concern in the law and in social practice has been that surrounding whiteness (Haney Lopez 1996; Dominguez 1994). Whiteness, at various times in our history, has been a prerequisite for citizenship, employment, adequate housing, land ownership, and education. Legal and social decisions about whether a particular group could be considered white have had tremendous material consequences, and the inequalities engendered by such arbitrary decisions have persisted for generations. Both African and Asian Americans have consistently fallen outside the color line encircling the definition of "whiteness" in America. Thus, the person with both white and African or both white and Asian ancestry embodies the sharpest contradiction of the racial system, which is why I deliberately chose individuals combining these particular heritages to interview for this book. I was concerned with the issues raised when the boundary of whiteness is transgressed and this transgression is made apparent in a person of mixed race (Tashiro 2002).

There are additional reasons for comparing the perspectives of those who have one black parent with those having one Asian parent. I was interested in beginning to identify some characteristics of the multiracial experience over the life course. However, to accomplish this, it was necessary to distinguish the effect of multiraciality from that of membership in the subordinate race alone. Studying two different groups offered the opportunity to do so. There have been both commonalties and differences in the racial rules as applied to people of African and Asian ancestry in the United States. Each minority group has had a unique collective history and location in the racial hierarchy. In the United States, the severest and most restrictive racial definitions have been applied to people of African ancestry (Tashiro 2002). In his detailed account of the evolution of the one-drop rule, or the rule of hypodescent, according to which anyone with a drop of African blood must be considered black, F. James Davis concludes, "This definition of who is black was crucial to maintaining the social system of white domination in which widespread miscegenation, not racial purity, prevailed" (1991, 62–63). People of various skin tones and mixtures of ancestry have been absorbed for generations into the African American community and culture (Tashiro 2002). This complicates the notion of a mixed race identity as distinct from an African American one in that so many African Americans have mixed ancestry but have been historically categorized, and have identified, as "Negro," "colored," or "black," depending on the era.

The situation for people of Asian ancestry has been somewhat different, although commonalties exist with the black experience. Discrimination against people of Asian ancestry in the United States has historically taken the form of exclusionary immigration, labor, and citizenship laws and practices based on race. These policies have fluctuated with labor needs and been differentially applied based on country of origin and sex (Espiritu 1997). As with mixed African Americans, historic evidence indicates that mixed Asian persons could not be considered white. This practice impacted their eligibility for citizenship (Tashiro 2002). Ian Haney Lopez (1996) describes the decision in *In re Knight* (1878), whereby Knight, who was half white, one-quarter Japanese, and one-quarter Chinese, was denied citizenship because a person of such mixed ancestry could not be considered white and was thus ineligible for citizenship. However, to my knowledge, there has been no consistently applied Asian American equivalent of the one-drop rule, by which any drop of Asian blood would render a person Asian. But, as Todd Sasaki's case illustrates, policies toward people of Asian ancestry could fluctuate dramatically. State relations with the country of origin and internal labor needs have heavily influenced U.S. policies toward Asians and Asian Americans. History does matter, and different patterns of identity and identification emerged for the two mixed race groups based on traditional differences in classification, which chapter 1 explores at length.

Participants were interviewed between one and three times, typically for one to two hours per session. Interviews were audiotaped and transcribed. The interviews were semistructured focused life histories, with broad questions about family history, the social milieu in which participants grew up, and memorable historic events combined with more focused questions about early memories of awareness of race, how race was dealt with in the family, race and everyday life, aging, identification, and influences on identity. Although I tried to recruit people through several means (advertising on the Internet, contacting a mixed race support group, and distributing flyers to multiracial organizations), by far my most successful avenues were my network of personal contacts and word of mouth. In contrast to my experience recruiting younger multiracials through the Internet, trust was a necessary precondition for these older mixed race Americans. Unless they knew who I was or knew someone who knew me, it was difficult to get them to talk to me about this topic.

The study included seven people of African American/white ancestry and thirteen people of Asian American/white background. The mixed Asian American group included people of Chinese, Filipino, and Japanese ancestry; they were of the first, second, and third generations of their families in the United States. Eleven women and nine men participated in the study. For the sake of brevity, I refer to the African American/white participants as "mixed African American" and to the Asian American/whites as "mixed Asian American" or as "mixed Chinese," "mixed Filipino," or "mixed Japanese." Participants' family backgrounds were primarily working-class. The participants themselves included members of the working class and professionals.

Most of the people I interviewed were living in the San Francisco Bay Area at the time of the study, although about half grew up in other parts of the United States or in Asia. The Bay Area is unique in ways that are relevant to the topic of mixed race. The population is extremely diverse to the point that certain of its cities, like Oakland and San Francisco, have no majority racial/ethnic population. However, much of the growth of racial minorities in this area has occurred in the last forty years, particularly among the Asian and Latino populations. Although many generations of African Americans,

Asians, and Latinos have lived in the region, when most of the people I interviewed were young, whites comprised the majority in most cities and certainly held political power.

The Bay Area also has a history of radical activity and a generally liberal political atmosphere. It has long been a promising site for organized resistance on the part of many constituencies: consider, for example, organized labor in the San Francisco general strike of 1934; students in the Free Speech Movement at the University of California, Berkeley, in 1964; students of color in the Third World strike at San Francisco State in 1968 and the Third World Liberation Front at the University of California, Berkeley, in 1969, which resulted in the establishment of ethnic studies departments; and radical African Americans in the founding of the Black Panther Party in Oakland in 1966. Undoubtedly, this history and the liberal atmosphere of the area influenced how my participants thought about what it means to be of mixed race.

However, it would be misleading to portray the Bay Area as an idyllic place for people of color. The gains they now experience were hard won through the struggles that took place in the 1950s and 1960s. Many of the interviewees confronted blatant institutionalized racism, such as school tracking by race and segregated housing. For example, Louise Soriano, a mixed Filipino American born in 1931, described how real estate agents refused to show property to her and her husband beyond a narrow strip that included Asian Americans, forming a buffer zone between the black and white parts of the city of Berkeley in the 1950s. The people in this book describe a social and political environment that would be unrecognizable in the environment of today's Bay Area.

That said, I make no claims that the particular people I interviewed represent all people of mixed race of this age in the United States. The study's focus in the San Francisco Bay Area and the fact that personal contacts and word of mouth formed my most successful recruitment methods undoubtedly influenced the representativeness of the group. It was not my purpose to generalize my findings from a representative sample to a population, and I make no claims in that regard. Rather, I wanted to investigate and explore the meaning of racial identity for the people I talked with and to let their stories speak for themselves. There are variations of age, race, nationality, sex, geographic origin, sexual orientation, disability, class, education, and political ideology among the twenty people I interviewed. I was interested in the complex ways different aspects of social location might interact with and give meaning to their experiences of being of mixed race. This book is organized to highlight the significance of family, race, class, gender, age, and nationality in how they experienced and interpreted being of mixed race.

Older Adults: The Missing Population in Mixed Race Research

My belief upon entering this research was that variation in social conditions across time and space influences subjectivity. I believed that racial identity, like race, is produced socially and, therefore, will vary with different norms, definitions of race, and attitudes. Individuals are inextricably influenced by the social milieu of the historical times in which they live (Elder 1995; Elder 1998). Choosing to study the question of mixed race identity in older people offered the possibility of historicizing their responses (Dien 2000). Interviewing people who had experienced different eras in terms of relevant structures like segregation, antimiscegenation laws, and definitions of race offered a chance to glimpse how those structures might have influenced something as simultaneously personal and collective as racial identity.

In the late 1990s, when I conducted the interviews for this book, the majority of the published research on people of mixed race concentrated on children, adolescents, and young adults and focused on identity issues primarily from a psychological perspective. Many of these studies seemed to assume that mixed race identity should be resolved by early adulthood. Kerry Rockquemore, David Brunsma, and Daniel Delgado (2009), in their review of approaches to mixed race identity, place authors from this period in the "variant" perspective (Thornton 1996), meaning that they affirm mixed race identity rather than taking the position that the biracial person should identify with one or the other heritage, which these authors call the "equivalent" perspective. Both the equivalent and variant approaches envision the achievement of a stable identity in early adulthood. As a mixed race person with a history, this assumption of an eventual static identity seemed terribly simplistic to me.

These early models of mixed race identity development also presumed the achievement of identity resolution to be an internal psychological process, giving minimal attention to the influence of structural forces and the power of recognized group identities. In my experience, the effects of power shifts, social movements, and changing representations of race on subjective self-identification have been enormous. Studying older people of mixed race offered the possibility of recovering through memory the effects of past historical circumstances on subjectivity. Older people of mixed race are living witnesses to history that has gone largely unstudied from the perspective of the individual human life. In the present, they carry within themselves the imprint of prior historical times. This is recoverable through memory via the interpretive filter of the present.

Since the original interviews were done, mixed race research has grown exponentially in complexity and sophistication. However, the populations studied have been overwhelmingly adolescents and young adults. Much larger samples have been analyzed, allowing for the observation of different manifestations of identity and, most importantly, the contextual factors that influence it (Rockquemore and Brunsma 2002; Rockquemore, Lasyloffy, and Noveske 2006; Harris and Sim 2002; Herman 2004; Cheng and Lively 2009). For example, in their research on black/white biracials, Rockquemore and Brunsma (2002) correctly place much more emphasis on the context of identification, such as the social networks and socialization experiences of the biracial person. In their review of theoretical models of biracial identity, Rockquemore and Brunsma found basically four options: singular, in which the biracial person identifies exclusively with one heritage (usually black); border, an exclusively blended biracial identity; situational variation; and a transcendent "human" identity. In their more recent review of theoretical approaches to multiracial identity, Rockquemore, Brunsma, and Delgado (2009) settle on a fourth position, the ecological approach, in which identity is influenced by context with no fixed endpoint. Based on the more recent research from larger data sets, they assert that racial identity often changes over the life course but, recalling Maria Root, not in a linear fashion. Social, cultural, and spatial context are key variables that influence identity. Significantly, the authors distinguish between racial identity, racial categories, and racial identification. Though the population they studied is much younger, their unpacking of the meaning of mixed race identity resonates with the dimensions of identity displayed by the people I interviewed.

Among studies using qualitative methods, Kendra Wallace (2001) provides a very rich picture of the complexities of identity negotiation for fifteen high school and university students of mixed heritage, between the ages of fifteen and thirty, using a novel technique with four visual representations of where the participants felt they fit with regard to their various heritage communities. "Home base/visitor's base" refers to those who felt grounded mostly in one side and might occasionally "visit" the other. "Life on the border" reflects not necessarily a choice but placement by others in a "liminal status." Those who chose "both feet in both worlds" were primarily high school students, raising questions about whether this is more possible at that age or for people who have come of age in the era in which the research was conducted. The option Wallace calls "shifting identity gears" is quite similar to what I call "situational racialization of feeling," explored in chapter 3, in which identity varies with context. None of Wallace's respondents identified solely with one group, and almost all identified with at least two of the graphics.

Age Matters

I was particularly interested in studying people of mixed heritage who were born during the times when antimiscegenation laws prevailed in many states. While most of the people I interviewed did not have living parents, all were very aware of the obstacles their parents faced. They have vivid memories of their parents' stories. Because I always asked them to start by describing how their parents got together, their stories connect us to an even more distant past. Since the oldest person I interviewed was ninety-four, some of what was described occurred more than a century ago. Their stories provide a living link to previous generations of individuals who faced considerable obstacles and hardships to marry across racial lines.

Life-course stage during key historical transitions clearly influenced how people of different ages thought about and experienced being of mixed race. This is explored in chapter 6. What was happening in the country and the world during the formative years of late adolescence and young adulthood played a particularly significant role in attitude and identity formation. Several participants described

pivotal events that shaped the meaning of minority group membership for them. The 1960s seemed to be a key watershed. Those who
came of age before the 1960s talked about identity and identification
differently from those who came of age during or after the 1960s.
Events from the mid-1960s to the early 1970s, when many of the gains
of the civil rights movement were being realized, had a particularly
profound impact. Several people also revealed how their definitions
of self and attitudes about aspects of their heritages changed with the
process of aging, which entails a complex interaction between internal
development and external social change.

Mixed Race Identity: The Racial Chimera

In discussing the primacy of race in America, Howard Winant (1994)
observes that to be without race is to be in danger of lacking an
identity. Since racially mixed people are often difficult to pigeonhole
by race, the question of identity always comes up for them. Often
as not, their first encounters with this issue come through the comments of others, questions and remarks like "What are you?" "Are
they adopted?" and "You don't look like ..." The fact that this type of
identity dissonance is imposed externally on the mixed race person
is a critical point.

But what is racial identity? In popular discourse, the question of
racial identity is still predominantly associated with only part of the
population: those who are "raced," that is, those who are not white.
We don't usually associate "racial identity" with whites, except perhaps
in the self-conscious propaganda of organized white supremacist
groups. We don't question the racial identities of whites or of people
who are born to two parents of the same racial group, although the
reality of the supposed purity of the groups we call "races" is spurious,
as has been pointed out so clearly by Rainier Spencer (2006). But
racial identity comes up for people like those in this book because
they embody a supposed dichotomy between the purity of whiteness
and color. They violate core beliefs of the bedrock ideology of race in
America: that race is biologically real, the races are mutually exclusive and distinct with intrinsic characteristics and worth, that race is
a property of those who are not white, and that a symbolic boundary
around whiteness constitutes the color line (Omi and Winant 1994;

Tashiro 2005). The ideology of race is about power. Racial identity, hence mixed race identity, is thus directly influenced by power: the power to categorize, to assign inherent meaning and worth to those categories, to shape representations of the people who inhabit them, and to allocate rights and resources based on race. When the people in this book were growing up, that power was manifested in every aspect of life via the color line.

I argue that for mixed race people who embody the contradiction of whiteness and color, making a consistent and coherent identity out of such requirements will remain challenging as long as the ideology of race persists, dividing us into distinct racial groups. As Naomi Zack (1995) points out, if black is defined as anyone with a drop of African ancestry, and white is defined as anyone without a drop of color, there is no logical place for the notion of mixed race. Problems with mixed race identity have to do with the fact that mixed race people are constantly struggling with society's racial essentialisms. The stories of the people in this book provide unique insights into how race operates in America from the perspectives of people who are at the epicenter of its contradictions.

As I entered this project, my interest focused on how the participants experienced identity and the factors that influenced those experiences. I sometimes felt that I was dealing with ever expanding, intersecting circles of influence as I attempted to understand and analyze what people said about identity. I found that racial identity for the older mixed race people in this book is not a singular entity but a multidimensional collage of responses to situations. However, I also found that there were limits to identity options, particularly for African Americans. Also, there were age differences associated with the way people responded.

Race and identity are not just about color but about sensibilities, depth, experiences, identification, empathy, resonance, inspiration, and imagination. Oftentimes, people formed complicated affinities beyond the official categories of their ancestries. They expressed their feelings about identity in ways that might seem contradictory if we conceive of racial or ethnic identity as fixed and singular. For example, Mary Ignacio, a mixed Filipina born in 1944, who at first glance looks Middle Eastern or Hispanic with her jet-black hair and striking profile, said of being asked to self-identity, "I would never say that I'm white. I don't think of myself as white. But I don't think of myself as Filipina. I mean, actually, in a way I think of myself as more Filipino than white. But I don't—it's very confusing—but I don't think of myself as culturally Filipino. I mean, I'm definitely Filipino and white. I mean, actually, I don't identify with white at all, identity-wise. But culturally, I do identify." In other parts of the interview, she also described herself as "feeling white all the time, in a way," as well as feeling mixed.

The mixed African Americans all included "black" or "colored" as one of the ways they identified. Yet, many of their narratives contained contradictory messages as well. For example, Brian Mitchell, a mixed African American man born in 1939, while casually speaking of himself as black several times in the interview also said, "My identity has really emerged out of the various kinds of living environments I've been in. I mean, if you asked me what I am, racially I'd say black, white, and Indian. But because I've never been totally one or the other, what's emerged is basic to my way of coping and dealing. So I don't identify. If anything, I would be—my behavior patterns and so forth would be more—would have to be white, since that's the environment I've lived in. I've never lived, with the exception of a couple months, in an all-black environment."

Mary's and Brian's remarks about identity and identification fracture commonplace notions of a solitary racial or ethnic identity. Cultural conditioning can be at odds with ascribed racial identity. Seemingly contradictory identifications can coexist. Listening to the stories in this book challenges our concepts of race and identity at the core. Early psychological models of racial identity and mixed race identity that envisioned identity development along a defined trajectory, culminating in resolution with one identity by adulthood, seem terribly simplistic when judged against the complexities of identity shared by the people described here.

Fairly early in the process of analyzing the interviews, I noticed that people like Mary and Brian talked about identity and identification in different ways. Some had to do with how they were identified *by* others. Sometimes they referred to how they identified themselves to others. Within the same interview, they might then name another way that they truly identified. And, like Todd Sasaki's feeling Jewish during the Six Day War in 1968, their feelings were at times episodically racialized in response to particular events and situations. Racial identity has multiple dimensions, some of which are stable and some of which fluctuate with the situation and historical context. In chapter 3, I sort participants' comments into five dimensions of racial identity: cultural identity, ascribed identity, identification to others, identification to self, and situational racialization.

Theorizing Mixed Race Subjectivity

In this book, I have attempted to show the relationship between structural influences and identity, or, more basically, between power and subjectivity. Here, I want to acknowledge some of theoretical frameworks that I found helpful. Setting the overall context for the position of mixed race people is what Michael Omi and Howard Winant (1994) call the "racial dictatorship" of the United States, referring to the fact that, for most of recorded U.S. history, racial apartheid has been supported by the rule of law. The legacy of the racial dictatorship is that we live with three important consequences that are significant for this study: the defining of American identity as white, the organization of a color line, and the essentializing of previously diverse groups into "races."

Mixed race people who are half white, like the people in this book, represent an affront to all three of Omi and Winant's consequences of the racial dictatorship. As such, they experience those consequences in unique ways. They violate the color line division. They embody the contradictions of racial essentialisms. Much of the "betwixt and between" feelings of mixed race people are produced by social expectations that are based on reactionary commonsense conceptions of mutually exclusive racial groups. The legacy of the racial dictatorship affects them in deep and contradictory ways. This is most demonstrated in my study by the different dimensions of racial identity participants express. They are particularly vulnerable to racial essentialisms and to challenges to their authenticity.

But how does this translate into the meaning of racial identity? Stuart Hall, a seminal figure in British cultural studies, offers a unifying perspective that emphasizes the subjective effects of the workings of power on identity. He emphasizes the effects of changing power relations on the discourses and representations of race that directly influence subjectivity. Theorizing identity is Hall's central project, but for him it is historically situated. Discourses of race vary historically, as do representations. Representations of race demonstrate the intersecting and mutually constitutive character of race, class, and gender, discussed in chapter 4. Changing representations also reflect fluctuations in power, as well as changes in hegemonic strategies. Thus, by necessity, in Hall's paradigm, identity is not fixed or essential. It is always defined in relationship to difference. However, its fluidity is not random but is directly related to the complex workings of power at global, national, and local levels.

Turning our attention to individual actors, the symbolic interactionist sociologists and their American pragmatist predecessors focus more on the microprocesses through which people construct identity. Like Hall, they emphasize the situational nature of identity, based as it is on the processes of social interaction. However, they are less concerned with the structural underpinnings that frame social interaction and give more attention to the specific actions people take to negotiate and renegotiate identity. Their work provides a framework for interpreting the processes mixed race people go through to create identity. This perspective is particularly relevant to the specific strategies people described using to "perform" race for the particular group they were trying to fit in with (Goffman 1959). In addition, the classic work of Charles Horton Cooley ([1902] 1993) on the reflected self and George Herbert Mead's ([1929] 1993) vision of the self as a social structure emphasize that there can be multiple selves arising out of the various social processes to which individuals are exposed, which is confirmed by the dimensions of identity expressed by the people in this book.

Finally, I found utility in the life-course perspective as an explanatory framework for interpreting the intersection of history and age and differences in perspectives on identity between age cohorts. The life-course perspective situates individual lives within historical time and place and acknowledges the significance of developmental stage for key experiences (Elder 1995, 1998).

Additional Themes

In addition to the material previously discussed on history (chapter 1), aging (chapter 6), and identity (chapter 3), the book is organized around major themes that include case studies about and analysis of the particular challenges of mixed race families, the complicated ways that race, class, and gender intersect with mixed race identity, and transnational experiences.

Chapter 2 evolved out of what I heard in response to my first interview question: "Tell me how your parents got together." Most of the parents of the people interviewed got together before the last laws prohibiting interracial marriage were struck down by the 1967 Supreme Court decision in *Loving v. Virginia.* Disbelief in familial relationships by others, denial, and even abandonment haunt the stories of the people in this book. In general, the hardships did not end with marriage for those who overcame the odds to wed across the color line. Frequently, they and their families faced discrimination in employment and housing, harassment from the police, ostracism by the white family of origin, and sometimes violence. Even after marriage, the legitimacy of their unions could be challenged. Intrafamilial relationships were inevitably affected by the racial inequality of the parents, and some families were not able to cope with the overwhelming difficulties of staying together. These narratives are rich with detail about what was risked in establishing liaisons that crossed the color line when such behavior was illegal and stigmatized and how racial inequality entered into everyday family life. Such material has rarely been published. I provide a case study of two mixed African American women, exploring how family life influenced their experiences of being mixed.

The intersections of race, class, and gender with mixed race are discussed in chapter 4. I examine the differences and similarities between the mixed African and Asian Americans. For example, several of the factors that influenced identity and identification for mixed Asian Americans were potential markers of foreignness, such as language and accent, factors that weren't present in the mixed African American interviews. One factor the mixed African Americans mentioned much more than the mixed Asian Americans was "lack of choice." While most of the mixed African Americans mentioned multiple ways of identifying, all included "black" or "colored" as one of those identities. Class and gender interacted with race in different ways for the two groups. Several of the mixed African American men experienced extreme vigilance from whites about their dating choices when they reached adolescence. For some of the mixed Asian American men, social class "colored" the ways they thought about racial identity.

Chapter 5 focuses on the mixed Asian Americans who spent significant years in other countries. Their accounts of life in Hong Kong, China, Japan, and the Philippines provide a contrast with mixed race life in the United States. Louise Soriano's story, which spans the Midwest, California, and the Philippines, where she barely survived the Japanese occupation during World War II, illustrates many of the complicated and contradictory aspects of being racially mixed in Asia. The lingering effects of Western colonialism in Asia complicated attitudes toward people of mixed race, and these participants described a variety of advantages and disadvantages to being mixed. One common thread between being of mixed race in Asia and the United States was the belief in white (or Western) dominance and superiority.

Finally, in chapter 7, I review the major themes of the book and discuss the possibilities for a coherent mixed race identity. I conclude that only true racial equality, coupled with societal awareness of differences of history and culture, can resolve the identity dilemmas of mixed race people. The contradictory expectations and representations projected onto people of mixed race are directly related to the state of race in America.

Note

1. All names are pseudonyms unless otherwise indicated.

1

History Matters

Racial Rules for Blacks and Asians

We are all in the midst of history, but we generally aren't aware of how the external context of the present moment is shaping our lives. Part of the problem may be that we tend to see history as being about major events, not the things that we can take for granted because of when and where we live. For example, I take for granted the fact that I, as a native-born mixed Asian American, can be an American citizen, own property, and live anywhere I can afford. Yet, none of these options would have been available to me a bit more than a century ago. I rarely think about this fact. Yet, my life has surely been shaped by the Supreme Court's 1898 decision in *United States v. Wong Kim Ark,* which upheld the Fourteenth Amendment to the U.S. Constitution by ruling that all people born on U.S. soil have the right to citizenship (Odo 2002). There are laws that appear in history books, and there are the day-to-day experiences shaped by those laws. When I speak of the impact of history, I refer to the complex relationships between the law, significant historical events, and how these phenomena intertwined with and shaped the lives of the people I interviewed. For example, the fact that the parents of many of my respondents got together when it was illegal to do so in most states conveyed an aura of illegitimacy to their marriages, which profoundly affected the stability of their families.

Tracing relevant history for the lives of people of color to a great extent involves examining legal decisions. Work in the tradition of critical race theory shows the fluctuating nature of racial categories and the effects legal changes have had on the subsequent treatment of people of various ancestries (Crenshaw 1995; Haney Lopez 1996; Odo 2002; Hickman 2003; Gross 2003). Legal decisions have been extremely significant for the lives of both Asian and African Americans. They have made the difference in whether one could become a citizen, whether one could vote, where one could live and work, whom one could marry, and whether it was possible to establish a family. In other words, they influenced every aspect of life. Identity cannot be separated from such profoundly important facets of everyday life. In this chapter I present a brief summary of themes and events from African American and Asian American history that are relevant to interracial families and their offspring. I give some examples of how historical legacies affected the families of the people in my study.

African and Asian Americans:
Some Commonalties of History

In *Strangers from a Different Shore,* Ronald Takaki (1989) tells the stories of Asian immigrants to the United States using archival sources to paint vivid portraits of the conditions they experienced. The first great wave of Asian immigration to the United States occurred in the territory of Hawaii in the 1870s. In his account, Takaki (1989, 25) quotes a memorandum to a plantation manager in Hawaii in 1890 acknowledging orders for

> bonemeal
> canvas
> Japanese laborers
> macaroni
> Chinamen

When I read this list, I recalled a similar one I saw on a visit to South Carolina in 1997. During that visit, I went on a tour of Boone Plantation, picking it because it had the least offensive advertisements of the plantations near Charleston. As part of the tour of the main house, our guide brought us into the "gentlemen's" smoking room. She called our attention to a piece of paper posted on the wall. It was a list of supplies to be purchased in town, something like a contemporary grocery list. Along with orders for several pounds of coffee, sugar, and flour appear the words "One negro girl" with a corresponding price.

Such mundane artifacts as these two lists tell us a great deal about how people of Asian and African descent were viewed in the United States. Being put on a grocery list implies that, like a sack of flour, one is a thing and therefore less than human. Being less than human, the labor of African and Asian Americans could be more vigorously exploited. It would not be exaggerating to say that these two groups would not have been tolerated in the United States were it not for the great need for their labor and its enormous profitability. Be it in sugar harvesting, cotton production, rice cultivation, mining, or the building of the railroads, much of this country's wealth was accumulated through the labor of people of color. The histories of African and Asian Americans are inextricable from the basic economies of the United States.

In particular, the role of black slavery was integral to the history and economic development of the United States. Steven Steinberg (1981) points out how essential the cotton trade was to the development of the economies of both the North and the South, documenting in detail how cotton provided the United States with its first and most significant export staple. In addition to supplying British textile industries, cotton provided the basis for the growth of the textile industry in the U.S. North. The capital generated by these economic transactions formed the basis of the rapid economic growth of the United States as a whole at a key point in its development. And slave labor was the foundation on which the country's economic development rested. An ideology was needed to justify this practice that was so profitable to the country as a whole. As Steinberg states, "It is facile to think that blacks were enslaved because they were defined as inferior; it would be closer to the truth to say that they were defined as inferior so that they might be enslaved" (1981, 30). He notes that the ideology of racial inequality that justified black enslavement would profoundly influence the treatment of others considered as racial and ethnic minorities.

Concomitant with the end of slavery achieved by the Civil War, expansion in the West and in Hawaii brought a mounting need for other sources of cheap labor (Okihiro 2001). This need, the particular conditions in the Asian countries of origin, and fluctuating quotas by and large accounted for the structure of Asian immigration in the nineteenth through the mid-twentieth centuries.

Steinberg correctly posits that the ideology justifying black slavery set the stage for the treatment of others viewed as not-white. While Asian immigrant workers were not slaves, they often labored under inhumane conditions and for wages that barely afforded subsistence. Many, such as the Chinese who built the western half of the Central Pacific Railroad, worked in the most hazardous conditions and died in much greater proportions than their white counterparts (Chan 1991). As members of contract labor gangs, they could essentially be sold and sent to work for the purchaser of their labor, having little choice in the matter. Many were kept in constant debt by company stores, thus unable to escape the prison of contract labor. Subhuman treatment was justified by the ideology of white supremacy, which was so well developed in the time of black enslavement.

The fact that both African and Asian Americans were valued solely for their labor and seen as inferior to whites influenced every aspect of their lives. However, these basic points of commonalty were translated differently for the two groups. Differences between the requirements of slavery versus contract labor, the status of the country of origin, and shifting definitions of racial group membership all played a part in the evolving histories of these groups and the treatment of their mixed offspring.

African American History, the Construction of Race, and Mixed Race

Some of the earliest people of African ancestry to arrive in what is now the United States were not slaves but indentured servants who arrived in Jamestown in 1619 (Franklin and Moss 1994). In the colonial world, racial boundaries and definitions were not immediately distinguished. Early interracial liaisons between blacks and whites commonly occurred between white indentured servants and blacks, both free and enslaved. The line between indentured servitude and enslavement was not so clearly drawn in the colonial world, and blacks and whites frequently worked in close proximity. The law treated the first people of mixed ancestry with some ambiguity for about the first fifty years in colonial Virginia. By 1662, the Virginia assembly had passed its first acts against miscegenation (Higginbotham and Kopytoff 2003; Feagin 2006). Mixed children of slave mothers were considered slaves, and consorting with "a negro man or woman" became a punishable act for any white person (Williamson 1995). However, liaisons between black men and white women aroused the most anxiety. Since the mothers were free, it was more difficult to make the argument that their mixed race children should not be. Severe penalties against white women who consorted with blacks and forced servitude of their mixed offspring were invoked as a disincentive to this type of interracial sex. At the same time, the more common unions between white slave masters and overseers and black female slaves were ignored and resulted in offspring who could be considered slaves (Fredrickson 1981).

The classification and treatment of mixed people of African ancestry was by no means uniform before 1850. Communities of free people of color existed in Louisiana and South Carolina (Dominguez 1994). However, there was never a third category that uniformly defined the position of people of mixed African ancestry throughout the United States.

In comparing the treatment of mixed offspring in the United States and in the West Indies and South Africa, where they occupied a third, intermediate stratum, George Fredrickson (1981) attributes the difference primarily to expedience. For example, in the West Indies, where small numbers of whites needed to control large slave populations, the creation of an intermediate stratum to carry out the overseer role was advantageous. In contrast, in the colonial South, there were enough free whites to play this role, and it was advantageous to elevate lower-class whites rather than mulattos to manage slaves. Promoting an ideology of racial inequality, which placed whites at the top of the hierarchy, thus counterbalanced potential class resentments by working-class whites toward the wealthier owners of slaves and property.

Though some relaxation of the racial divide occurred during the post–Civil War Reconstruction era, a resurgence of white supremacy in the late nineteenth century resulted in the reinstitution of antimiscegenation laws and a more rigorous definition of whiteness. Although slavery had ended, second-class citizenship for blacks had not. During Reconstruction, southern blacks had been able to vote and hold political office in most states. However, economic stability was not achieved for newly freed slaves. In addition, white supremacists began organizing almost immediately after the Civil War ended. The combination of continued economic domination and the proliferation of virulent white supremacist ideology allowed the rollback of the gains of Reconstruction state by state. With the removal of the last federal troops from the South in 1877, the stage was set for the triumph of white supremacy. State conventions systematically rewrote their constitutions to effectively disenfranchise blacks by a plethora of requirements such as poll taxes, tests based on the ability to read and understand documents like the U.S. Constitution (subject to the interpretation of the test administrator), and property ownership. With the 1896 Supreme Court ruling upholding segregation in *Plessy v. Ferguson,* strict segregation in all walks of life and rigid enforcement of the color line between black and white were institutionalized throughout the South (Franklin and Moss 1994). With the disenfranchisement of blacks, consolidation of control could proceed, and the American version of apartheid became institutionalized in the Jim Crow era (Feagin 2006).

The Delany sisters, two African American women aged 102 and 104 at the time their autobiography *Having Our Say* (1993) was published, remember their childhood before and after Jim Crow: "When we got to Pullen Park, we found changes there, too. The spring where you got water now had a big wooden sign across the middle. On one side, the word 'white' was painted, and on the other, the word 'colored.' Why, what in the world was all this about? We may have been little children but, honey, we got the message loud and clear. But when nobody was looking, Bessie took the dipper from the white side and drank from it" (Hearth, Delany, and Delany 1993, 95–96). The separate but equal doctrine was maintained in many states until the 1954 Supreme Court decision in *Brown v. Board of Education of Topeka,* which outlawed segregated public schools. The period of legal segregation also saw the flourishing of antimiscegenation laws (Pascoe 1996) and the most extreme hysteria about identifying who was "truly white" and who had "hidden blackness" in his or her family tree (Williamson 1995). Rigorous attention to racial classification was the mechanism for maintaining a social order built on racial hierarchy. By the beginning of the twentieth century, with the consolidation of Jim Crow, most southern states were using the one-drop rule of hypodescent, meaning that any African ancestry whatsoever resulted in a person's being classified as black. A two-category system became codified, in which children of mixed black and white parentage were considered black (Feagin 2006).

As a result, according to Joel Williamson, the mulatto population (which included individuals mixed with any degree of African ancestry, by his definition) that had been moving in the direction of whiteness turned to blackness out of necessity. As Williamson states, "Because the great majority of American Negroes are in fact of mixed ancestry, and because mulattos and pure blacks came ultimately to fuse their cultural heritages, what begins in the colonial period as mulatto history and culture ends in the twentieth century as Negro history and culture" (1995, xii). Thus, a population with a variety of different ancestries became essentialized as black through the hegemony of the one-drop rule. The historical legacy of the rule of hypodescent with its extreme definition of blackness was still enormously significant for how the mixed African Americans I interviewed define themselves and were defined by others (Spencer 2006).

All of the mixed African Americans I interviewed talked about the presence of this legacy in their lives. For example Helen Wilson, a mixed African American woman born in 1932, spoke of the perceived normalcy of growing up in segregated Galveston as all she knew, something you didn't question in her time. As she said, "In Texas the schools were segregated, and I went to a segregated grammar school. We knew that's the way it was." Although light skinned, with Caucasian and Native American ancestry, she and her family were subjected to the rigid definition of the color line, and "the family was so many different colors, from very, very fair to real dark, you know. But everybody just accepted that."

Jim Crow was most entrenched in the South, and economic opportunities were slim there for African Americans. During and after World War I, the African American population became increasingly urbanized with large-scale migration to the cities in search of employment. World War II brought about new opportunities for African Americans. For example, President Franklin D. Roosevelt's Fair Employment Executive Order of 1941 prohibited discrimination in employment in the defense industries. Along with other Americans seeking work, thousands of African Americans migrated to areas with defense jobs, such as the major California coastal ports. During wartime, the total black population of the San Francisco Bay Area expanded by over 227 percent (Johnson 1993). Many of the new black migrants to the area settled in the East Bay city of Oakland, where the parents of some of the people I interviewed sought economic opportunities. This pattern was not confined to African Americans. Sam Cole, a mixed African American born in 1944, recounts how his white mother and grandfather came to the Bay Area from Chicago. "They came out here, my mom and my grandpa at the end of 1942, to work at the Kaiser shipyards in Richmond. My mom was a welder in the ships. And like so many women, she made way better money than she had [before]."

There was much more freedom in California than in the South, where the majority of the new black population came from, and blacks and whites were thrown into much closer contact than would have been possible under segregation. However, as blacks replaced Asians as the largest racial minority, due in part to the relocation of the Japanese population during World War II, racial bias toward blacks grew (Johnson 1993, 55).

The 1950s and 1960s saw unprecedented organized resistance and action on the part of the black population and its allies, coupled with historically significant civil rights legislation. Some of the most memorable events included the Montgomery bus boycott of 1956 led by Reverend Martin Luther King Jr.; the desegregation of Central High School in Little Rock, Arkansas, in 1957, accomplished with the use of federal troops; the sit-in movement launched in 1960 in Greensboro, North Carolina; the freedom marches, culminating in the 1963 March on Washington for Jobs and Freedom; the Selma-to-Montgomery march of 1965; and the Poor People's Campaign of 1968.

Though racially mixed, several of the people I interviewed took part in the struggle for racial justice. Sam Cole talks about being swept up in the civil rights movement in the Bay Area: "And then we were having the Mel's drive-in sit-ins, 'cause Mel's was a segregated place. People glorify this Mel's stuff? Mel's was a place that we hated. So I became active, and there was one at Hi's drive-in here, where Carl's Junior is right down the street, that was a segregated place. Montgomery Wards was still segregated. We picketed there. My brother, who's the fairest skinned of us all with his big blue eyes, got spat on there, called a white-looking nigger." Being fair skinned clearly offered no protection from racism for Sam and his brother. In fact, Gregory Williams, of a similar age to Sam, describes the particularly virulent treatment he received as a "black" man who could pass for white in *Life on the Color Line* (1996), which discusses his life before and after his placement on the wrong side of the color line in Indiana. During this period, the color line was still actively maintained, and special vigilance was exercised toward "white-looking" men in particular who could potentially pass for white, explored more in chapter 4.

The farthest-reaching legislative accomplishment of this period was the passage of the Civil Rights Act of 1964, which prohibited discrimination and segregation in voting rights, public accommodation, public facilities, public education, and federally assisted programs and extended the life of the Commission on Civil Rights. Title VII of the act established the Equal Employment Opportunity Commission and is still the cornerstone of fair employment law. In addition, Executive Order 11246 established affirmative action to eliminate historical patterns of discrimination in employment. The Voting Rights Act of 1965 further strengthened the fight to remove obstacles to black political participation by giving the attorney general the power to intervene in cases of discriminatory voting requirements. The Fair Housing Act of 1968 prohibited discrimination in the sale, rental, or financing of housing. Several of these laws gave greater rights not just to African Americans but to other minorities and white women as well.

Of course, the fact that antidiscrimination laws were passed did not eliminate discrimination. The reaction against the improvement in rights for blacks was frequently violent. At the same time, there was growing impatience on the part of a new generation of militant black leaders with the slow pace of progress. The 1960s and 1970s saw the rise of the Black Power movement. There was a radical revisioning of the meaning of blackness, personified by the slogan "Black Is Beautiful," which reclaimed the pejorative word "black" as a symbol of pride and power.[1] Fred Johnson talks about being swept up in the movement for ethnic studies while at San Francisco State University and having the direction of his life changed: "I was sitting in an econ class, and these black guys came storming into the classroom and started talking all this shit about racism and stuff, and I had no idea what they were talking about.... But intuitively I knew that they were saying something that was true. And I went to a meeting, and the next thing you know, I was in the strike, and next thing you know, I was the chairman of the Legal Defense Fund. And I never went back to business."

This sentiment had a profound influence on other communities of color, which also organized around ethnic pride and fought alongside African Americans for the establishment of new programs, like ethnic studies departments in universities. When I moved to the Bay Area in the late 1960s, demonstrations by the Third World Liberation Front at the University of California, Berkeley, and the Third World Student Strike at San Francisco State University were in full swing. Coming from the East Coast, for the first time in my life I encountered a sizable, active Asian American movement in alliance with African Americans and other people of color for greater rights and representation.

Overview of Asian American History

Unlike that of African Americans, the history of Americans of Asian ancestry cannot be separated from immigration policy, which, in turn, has been inextricable from labor needs in the United States (Hing 1993; Espiritu 1997; Chan 1991; Glenn 2002). Until 1965, immigration from Asian nations was heavily regulated based on fluctuating requirements for cheap labor. The histories of the various Asian nationalities are interrelated because restrictions on immigration from one nation frequently resulted in the need to open it up to another. Also, by using Asian immigrants of different nationalities, labor solidarity could be weakened. This was particularly evident in Hawaii, where Japanese workers were brought in to compete with Chinese laborers and keep wages low (Takaki 1989).

Limitation of the rights of Asian Americans centered on their ineligibility for citizenship and all its associated privileges. As early as 1790, Congress restricted naturalization to "white persons," a constraint that remained in place until passage of the Immigration and Nationality Act of 1952 (Haney Lopez 1996). Thus, immigrants who were not considered white could never hope to obtain the benefits of citizenship. Immigration policy toward Asians did not change significantly until after World War II. In 1952, the McCarran-Walter Act eliminated racial barriers to naturalization and overturned the Naturalization Act of 1790 and its 1870 amendment, which had previously barred Asians from citizenship. However, it left intact the quota system from the 1924 Immigration Law. It created a new, restrictive "Asia-Pacific triangle" consisting of countries from India to Japan and restricted immigration from this region to a total of two thousand people annually. Enacted during the McCarthy period, this act also allowed for the deportation of any immigrant deemed "subversive."

The 1965 Immigration and Nationality Act represented a historic leap forward in U.S. policy toward non-European immigrants. For the first time, this amendment to the 1952 law placed a quota on immigration from the Western Hemisphere and abandoned all race-based immigration policies (Shinagawa and Jang 1998). It emphasized family reunification with relatives of American citizens or residents.

Further advances in immigration policy were made by the Immigration Act of 1990, which removed the emphasis on family reunification and increased the number of immigrants eligible to enter based on job skills or special contributions. In addition, many refugees have been admitted from Southeast Asia in the post-1965 period. These changes in immigration policy have radically altered the profile of Asian America. The new Asian immigrants include significant numbers of white-collar professionals, in contrast to the largely unskilled pre–World War II immigrants. The gender balance has also changed, with women comprising the majority of new Asian immigrants and many arriving as families (Espiritu 1997). There has been tremendous growth in populations that were small prior to 1965, including Vietnamese, Asian Indians, and Korean Americans. There has also been a large increase in Chinese immigrants. Because of the older ages of the people I interviewed, their nationalities reflect an earlier period of Asian immigration, when the majority of Asian Americans were of Chinese, Japanese, or Filipino ancestry. To provide historical context, some of the pertinent highlights of the histories of these three groups are next summarized.

Chinese Americans

The Chinese were the first Asian group to immigrate to the United States in large numbers, beginning in the mid-1800s (Hing 1993). Most were peasants driven to emigrate by the extreme poverty that existed in China at the time. The government of China during this period was forced to pay large sums to Western powers involved in the Opium Wars of 1839 to 1842 and 1856 to 1860, which they raised by imposing high taxes on the peasantry. Many peasants were unable to pay their taxes and lost their land. Peasants were particularly impoverished in Guangdong (Canton) province, which was the source of much of the Chinese migration (Takaki 1989; Corbett 2010).

Initially, there were few restrictions on Chinese immigration because of the growing demand for labor in mining, railroad construction, laundries, and domestic work. However, there was strong anti-Chinese sentiment on the mainland West Coast, particularly in California. In 1870, Congress voted to refuse to extend naturalization rights to Chinese. This, combined with an 1875 statute barring the entry of Chinese prostitutes (but used against almost all Chinese women), made the establishment of stable Chinese families and communities extremely difficult.

Anti-Chinese sentiment culminated in the Chinese Exclusion Act of 1882, which prohibited the entry of most Chinese laborers for ten years. It was extended several times and made indefinite in 1904. Only Chinese students and merchants were allowed to immigrate, and after the passage of the 1924 Immigration Act, even they became ineligible for citizenship. World War II resulted in a relaxing of the exclusion laws. The Chinese Exclusion Act was repealed in 1943, and in 1946 Chinese wives of American citizens were allowed to enter, unrestricted by the quota system. This right was extended to other Asian Americans by 1952. Between 1946 and 1965, the Chinese American population tripled. Between 1965 and 1990, the Chinese American population increased fivefold (Hing 1993).

Japanese Americans

The Japanese government restricted emigration of Japanese citizens prior to the 1880s (Spickard 1989). Passage of the Chinese Exclusion Act of 1882 and a concomitant need for cheap labor, coupled with the Japanese government's relaxation of emigration restrictions in 1885, resulted in significant Japanese immigration to work on the plantations of Hawaii. Immigration restrictions were applied less stringently to the Japanese than the Chinese because Japan was a rising military power in Asia with which the United States wanted to remain on good terms (Espiritu 1997). Although Japanese immigration was restricted,

Japanese men were able to send for wives, many of whom were "picture brides," in marriages arranged via letters and photographs.

The Gentleman's Agreement of 1907 between the governments of the United States and Japan limited, but did not totally eliminate, immigration of Japanese laborers. It did permit immigration of wives and children as well. As a result of more liberal policies toward the immigration of women, the Japanese American community did not suffer from the degree of gender imbalance experienced by Chinese and Filipino immigrants during this period. Some became successful in family farming. In response to the competition presented by the Japanese, California passed the Alien Land Law in 1913, which banned any noncitizens, such as the Japanese, from owning property. With the passage of the Immigration Act of 1924, all Asians became ineligible for citizenship, resulting in a sharp decline in Japanese immigration.

On February 19, 1942, President Roosevelt signed Executive Order 9066, ordering the internment of 120,000 persons of Japanese ancestry, primarily residents of the West Coast. This effectively disrupted and geographically dispersed Japanese communities. Geographic concentrations of Japanese Americans eliminated by internment were never reestablished after people were released from the camps. Unlike for most of the other Asian immigrant groups, the immigration reforms of 1965 have had a negligible effect on Japanese immigration. In contrast to the Chinese and Filipinos, the Japanese had been able to maintain a semblance of family structure in America, so family reunification was less of an issue. In addition, postwar economic growth in Japan lessened the incentive to emigrate. Because of its modest growth relative to other Asian American communities, the Japanese American population, which had been the largest in 1965, became the third largest by 1990 and was the least populous of the Asian subgroups identified in the U.S. census in 2010 (U.S. Census Bureau 2011).

Filipino Americans

The first Filipino American community was established in Louisiana in the 1500s by sailors who jumped ship from Spanish galleons in Mexico (Hing 1993). Filipino immigration differed in one fundamental way from that of the Japanese and Chinese. The 1898 war with Spain had resulted in U.S. annexation of the Philippines. As a result, Filipinos were granted special noncitizen status, which exempted them from immigration quotas.

In spite of their special status, Filipinos did not emigrate to the United States in significant numbers until the passage of the Gentleman's Agreement with Japan increased the demand for cheap labor, particularly in Hawaii. Filipino immigration grew precipitously until the Tydings-McDuffie Act of 1934, which, by establishing the Philippines as a commonwealth and guaranteeing future Philippine independence, rescinded the special status of Filipino immigrants as nationals. Many viewed this act as a thinly veiled mechanism for achieving Filipino exclusion. It also reduced to fifty the number of Filipinos permitted to immigrate yearly. In addition, deportation of Filipinos was encouraged by the allocation of public funds for their return to the Philippines, and Filipinos residing in the United States were reclassified as aliens.

As with the Chinese, World War II brought greater acceptance of Filipinos in America. Filipinos distinguished themselves alongside American troops in the Bataan Peninsula against the Japanese. At first excluded from the armed services, Filipino Americans agitated to join the fight against the Japanese and for the liberation of their homeland, and eventually President Roosevelt acceded to their wishes. Although they still faced discrimination, as members of the military Filipinos were allowed to become citizens (in theory). The immigration reforms of 1965 allowed enormous expansion of the Filipino American population, now one of the biggest Asian American groups in the United States.

The Construction of Race and Mixed Race for Asian Americans

While the rights associated with citizenship were based on whiteness, who was white was far from clear, and the boundaries of whiteness have shifted with changing ideologies of race and expediency (Dominguez 1994; Pascoe 1996; Haney Lopez 1996; Williamson 1995). Considerable confusion clearly existed about how to classify persons who were not obviously "white" or "black."

For example, Chinese were frequently assigned the same racial qualities associated with blacks. Similar mythologies assigned them hypersexuality and an unhealthy interest in white women. "A magazine cartoon depicted the Chinese as a bloodsucking vampire with slanted eyes, a pigtail, dark skin, and thick lips. Like blacks, the Chinese were described as heathen, morally inferior, savage, childlike, and lustful. . . . Chinese men were seen as sensuous creatures, especially interested in white women" (Takaki 1989, 101).

Of course, the relationship between alleged Chinese male interest in white women and immigration policy restricting the entry of Chinese women didn't seem to occur to anyone who was in a position to solve the "Chinese problem." The association of Asians with blacks persisted, and as recently as 1925, the Mississippi Supreme Court ruled that school segregation laws applying to the "colored race" prohibited children of Chinese ancestry from attending white schools (Loewen 1988).

Designation of racial status was crucial yet inconsistent; for example, Armenians were classified as "Asiatics" in California, thus ineligible for naturalized citizenship, until the 1909 *In re Halladjian* decision, which ruled that Armenians were Caucasians, giving them the right to own land (Haney Lopez 1996). At one point, Chinese were considered "Indians," therefore nonwhite, while Japanese were deemed "Mongolian," thus also ineligible for citizenship (Almaguer 1994). The issue of who could be considered as "white" or "not-white" was clearly not stable. However, the implications for access to resources and status were enormous depending on which side of that boundary one happened to fall.

Ian Haney Lopez's 1996 study of the racial prerequisite cases, which were individual challenges to the denial of citizenship based on the race of the plaintiff, offers insights into the construction of not-whiteness. The first such case, *In re Ah Yup*, was decided in 1878 and concerned the unsuccessful petition for citizenship of Ah Yup, denied on the basis that Chinese are not white. Judge Sawyer based his decision on the "scientific" categories of Johann Blumenbach[2] and others, as well as "common knowledge." He argued that Chinese are Mongolian, and the term *white person* has never included members of the Mongolian race. Essentially, all of the racial prerequisite cases based their challenges on claims to whiteness. Immigrants from Hawaii, China, Japan, Burma, and the Philippines, as well as mixed race Asian applicants, were denied citizenship on the basis of their not-whiteness. Mexicans and Armenians were deemed "white," and the courts reversed themselves, sometimes repeatedly, in their judgments about Syrians, South Asian Indians, and "Arabians." Invariably, people of Chinese, Japanese, and Filipino ancestry were denied their petitions based on being found not-white (Odo 2002). In cases of mixed Asian/white ancestry, such as *In re Knight,* who was half white, one-quarter Japanese, and one-quarter Chinese (Haney Lopez 1996), the plaintiffs were found to be not-white, reflecting the prevalent attitude that color outweighed whiteness taken to the extreme in the construction of the black/white color line. The effects of these legal decisions can be felt today in our current construction of racial classifications and our ideas about what makes a group a separate "race." They also had a profound impact on interracial relationships and mixed race families, explored in the next chapter.

Notes

1. I am simplifying a complex period in black history here. As Omi and Winant (1994) point out, the Black Power movement did not make a complete break with the civil rights movement. The Black Power movement embraced a broad range of political perspectives. Also, black nationalism did not begin in the 1960s; it had philosophical roots going back at least as far as the Garveyite movement of the 1920s.

2. Blumenbach divided humanity into five varieties with regional associations. They were Caucasian, Mongolian, Ethiopian, American, and Malay. The groups were ranked based on the degree of their civilized attributes. This was based on his theory of *degeneration,* according to which groups acquired their differences by exposure to different environmental conditions. Blumenbach originated the term *Caucasian* to refer to European whites because of his belief that the women of the Georgian region of the Caucasus were the most beautiful in the world (Schiebinger 1993). According to Blumenbach's theory, life began in the Caucasus, which could be proven because of the whiteness of the inhabitants' skin in that region. He theorized that the darker races represented a degeneration from pure whiteness.

2

Mixed Race

It's a Family Affair

Mixed race is inevitably a family affair, even if both parents were not physically present in the lives of their children. During the times when the parents of the people I interviewed got together, the white parents' transgression of the color line frequently resulted in drastic disruptions in connections with their families of origin and constant challenges to the legitimacy of their relationships with their spouses and partners of color.

The first question I asked of the people in this book was how their parents got together. Their responses provide a window into life when it was illegal for whites and people defined as not-white to marry. The parents of many of the people I interviewed had to engage in subterfuge, leave their state of residence, and risk imprisonment to "cross the line" of race in order to marry. It is difficult in today's environment to comprehend what these men and women had to go through just to be together. Yet, such events took place only a generation or two ago. In general, the hardships these parents faced did not end with their marriages. Frequently, they and their families endured discrimination in employment and housing, harassment from the police, ostracism by the white family of origin, and sometimes violence. Even after marriage, the legitimacy of their union could be challenged. In addition, a persistent theme runs through these stories involving challenge and denial of familial blood ties between parents and children. Yet, the majority of the families of the people I interviewed stayed together, which seems extraordinary given the obstacles they faced.

Historical Background on Mixed Race Families

Because of their ages, several of the people in this book were directly affected by historical attitudes and laws regarding miscegenation, and some of their comments and stories are interwoven into this section.

Beginning with their earliest histories in this country, African and Asian Americans encountered enormous obstacles to the formation of any semblance of family life. Families of black slaves were commonly separated at sale with the justification that family ties among slaves were loose or nonexistent (Franklin and Moss 1994). This was undoubtedly another case of developing a belief to justify an abhorrent practice, as their masters acknowledged that runaway slaves were frequently seeking reunification with their families. It was not unusual for young children to be sold, and some slave traders specialized in the market for them.

In addition, slaves were valuable property, and breeding them was quite lucrative. Thus, female slaves were esteemed for their child-bearing capabilities and encouraged to bear as many children as possible. Babies were worth $200, and young, male field hands could fetch prices as high as $1,800 by 1860 (Franklin and Moss 1994). Any children born to slaves were the property of the slave owner and could be sold or hired out at great profit. In some cases they were his own children. This was brought home most vividly to me, again during my visit to Boone Plantation in South Carolina. In the "gentlemen's" room that I mentioned in the previous chapter, a stairway led to the basement of the mansion. Our guide informed us that female slaves were kept in that area for the sexual use of the men of the family. The fact that slavery was such a profitable institution had a major influence on the categorization of mixed race children born from such liaisons and on the subsequent construction of race for African Americans (Fredrickson 1981).

Continued discrimination against African Americans after the abolition of slavery and well into the twentieth century often resulted in the dispersal of families, as potential wage earners migrated, particularly from the South, in search of opportunities (Franklin and Moss 1994; Johnson 1993). Limits on economic opportunities, lack of jobs, substandard segregated housing, and white hostility challenged family stability in the northern cities as well.

As with African Americans, racism and the supremacy of labor needs dictated policies that had a direct impact on sex, marriage, and family life for Asian Americans. As Yen Le Espiritu (1997) and Evelyn Nakano Glenn (2002) have pointed out, prior to World War II, treatment of Asian immigrants was highly gendered and aimed at reinforcing the temporary, labor-based status of the Asian immigrant male. The resulting extreme gender imbalance, coupled with antimiscegenation laws and restrictions on citizenship, enhanced the misery of largely male Asian immigrant populations on the U.S. mainland.[1]

For many male Asian immigrants, the shortage of women of their nationality led to intermarriage with other minority groups, the use of prostitutes, and often a lifetime of loneliness (Espiritu 1997). Some coped with this loneliness through the establishment of fictive kin networks. Espiritu states, "Missing the company of wives and small children, single Asian men adopted and were adopted by the few families that were around. In the Filipino community in Hawaii, as many as 200 men would be invited to be godparents at every religious ceremony, from baptism to marriage" (1997, 24). Thus, prior to the changing of immigration laws to allow more Asian women to enter, unlike the pattern of the post–World War II era, the intermarriage that did occur was usually between an Asian man and non-Asian woman, which is reflected in the profile of most of the parents of the older mixed Asian Americans I interviewed.

Beginning in 1907, as a further disincentive for women to wed Asian immigrants, any U.S. woman who married a noncitizen lost her citizenship and could be repatriated to her husband's country of origin. Jane Murakami, a mixed Japanese American woman born in 1916, remembered how her family was affected by this law. Jane's father was born in Japan and met her mother in California. Jane's father had always dreamt of coming to the United States to marry a blond, blue-eyed woman. Jane's mother, a woman of German ancestry, fit that picture. Although Jane's mother was born in San Francisco and was a U.S. citizen at the time of her marriage, she lost her citizenship because of her marriage to Jane's Japanese father. According to

Jane, "In those days, you couldn't marry an alien. My mother lost her citizenship because she married my father. That was terrible." When Jane herself decided to wed a U.S.-born Japanese American during the World War II years, she had to swear she was Japanese and not American in order to marry him. "So when I went to get a marriage license, the dumb form, the clerk in Oakland, he said, you can't marry him, he's Japanese. I said no, he's an American citizen. He was born in Alameda. He said, 'You have to swear that you're Japanese.' I said, I will swear I'm Japanese, but I'm an American citizen, just like you. How dumb the government—how could they do that?" Thus, Jane had to choose one side of her mixed ancestry in order marry the man she loved. The very notion of a mixed race identity was legally impossible for her.

I have described some of the challenges facing African and Asian Americans with regard to the formation of intimate relationships and families. When their familial relationships involved whites, as was the case with the parents of the people in this book, the challenges became even more daunting. In *White Men on Race,* based on interviews with powerful white men, Joe Feagin and Eileen O'Brien note, "A person's parents are usually determined by the racial practices of this society, such as the pressures to choose a mate from one's own racial group" (2003, 7). Feagin and O'Brien are referring to pressures that persist in contemporary times. How much greater was the pressure that existed prior to the rescinding of the antimiscegenation laws, when it was, in fact, illegal to marry outside of one's racial group in many states. The lingering disapprobation toward those who cross the color line to marry has deep historical roots.

As recently as 1930, twenty-nine of the forty-eight states had laws prohibiting white/black marriages. These laws were most prevalent in the South and West. The last antimiscegenation laws were not overturned until 1967, when the U.S. Supreme Court decision in the landmark *Loving v. Virginia* case ruled that state's antimiscegenation law unconstitutional (Pascoe 1996). Laws prohibiting interracial sex and marriage applied not just to blacks but to others considered not-white. While some antimiscegenation laws had existed in the colonial period, white hysteria about miscegenation reached a peak in the post-Reconstruction Jim Crow period and persisted well into the twentieth century.

Such hysteria extended to Asian/white miscegenation. Anti-miscegenation laws affecting Asians proliferated during the period from 1910 to 1950, even in areas with small Asian populations (Chin 2002). During this period, the Chinese and Filipino gender ratios were heavily weighted toward males. Filipino men married non-Filipino women, particularly of Mexican origin, more than the Chinese and Japanese. However, their reported consorting with white women most aroused anti-Filipino sentiment. In 1929, in an incident in Watsonville, California, precipitated by the sight of a Filipino man with a white teenage girl, hundreds of white men attacked a Filipino dance hall. In the ensuing riots, one Filipino was killed, and many more were beaten (Takaki 1989). According to Ronald Takaki, Filipino men had a reputation as better lovers than white men, which put them at particular peril for persecution. Takaki quotes from a number of colorful sources excoriating the predatory seductiveness of Filipino men, such as one Judge D. Rohrback, who blamed the Filipinos for the violence in Watsonville: "'Damn the Filipino! He won't keep his place,' the judge exclaimed in an interview. 'The worst part of his being here is his mixing with young white girls from 13 to 17, buying them silk underwear and . . . keeping them out till all hours of the night. And some of these girls are carrying a Filipino's baby around inside them.'" Fears of race mixing were at the heart of this hysteria. The aforementioned Judge Rohrback predicted that there would be "40,000 half-breeds in California within ten years if the 'Filipino problem'" went unchecked.

At the time, California law prohibited marriage between whites and "Negroes, mulattos, or Mongolians." While Filipinos were clearly "brown" and not "white," some ambiguity existed about whether they were included in the three prohibited categories. The law was successfully challenged in 1933 by Salvador Roldan on the grounds that, as a Filipino, he was Malayan, not Mongolian. However, almost immediately after this decision, the law was amended to include the "Malay race" in the restricted category (Takaki 1989).

Around the time of the Watsonville riot, the parents of Gus Pimental were preparing to enact Judge Rohrback's nightmare in rural California. Born in 1939 to a Filipino father and white mother, Gus painted a vivid picture of the perils of miscegenation. He first described his parent's love in romantic terms.

And this is the story my mom tells me. The truck drove, with all these Filipino workers, the truck drove by the house where my mother and her sister and her cousins lived, and my mother and father saw each other.... They went back to the same field the next day, and my mother waited for the truck, my father fixed himself in the truck so that he could see her. The eye contact was real. They made this wonderful eye contact. So lo and behold, Sunday came, and my mother and her family, which were very strict Spaniards, went to church and in the back of the church was my father, this Filipino farmworker, dressed in these real nice clothes. He had all his best duds on. And so that was the first Sunday. And then the next Sunday he came back again.

Although contact between unmarried women and men in this era was strictly chaperoned, Gus's parents somehow managed to exchange a few words and meet. When Gus's mother's parents discovered that she was seeing his father, she was sent away to live in another part of California. Eventually, Gus's father found her, and they decided to elope; they were married in Oakland. Gus is unclear about how they were able to wed, as marriage between Filipinos and whites was still prohibited in California at this time. Apparently, there was variation in the actual enforcement of antimiscegenation laws. When Gus's mother's family found out about the wedding, they called the sheriff in San Francisco. Gus described what followed: "When they got off the ferry boat from Oakland to San Francisco, the sheriff of San Francisco arrested my father. For white slavery. That was the charge. That was the charge. White slavery."

Gus's mother negotiated with her family and eventually got them to drop the charges on the condition that she would annul the marriage. When she did not follow through on her promise, Gus's mother's family essentially disowned her. Some aspects of the social world around Gus and his siblings as they grew up mirrored the hostility of his mother's family toward the marriage. Gus's parents and their growing family had difficulty finding landlords who would rent to a mixed couple. Eventually they settled in San Francisco's Fillmore District, already a mixed neighborhood with Japanese, Filipinos, blacks, and Jews, among others. Although the neighborhood was tolerant, Gus remembers individual acts of hostility toward the family in the city at large: "I remember this shit that we used to experience as kids of mixed race, you know. Getting on the bus and people would look at my mother and they'd look at my father and we'd walk by and white people would say, poor children, but they'd make sure we heard it. We'd walk by and I'm a little kid right at ear level, right, 'cause I'm only three foot something. They'd say in my ear, poor children."

As a result of being ostracized by the white side of the family, Gus and his siblings grew up as a part of the local Filipino community. Not surprisingly, Gus identifies first as Filipino due to the hostility of the white side of his family and the Filipino community's acceptance. His story shows the inextricability of his identity from his family's experiences of racism, both informal and legalized.

The legitimacy of marriages could be questioned. Particularly for some of the mixed African American/white families, this took the form of harassment by the police, described by both Grace Nelson and Kim Cole later in this chapter. Kim also described how the deed for family property had to be put in her white mother's name because of restrictions on property ownership for blacks and Asians. In the 1950s, when this event occurred, it would have been more typical for the male head of household to purchase the property. Such reversals of typical familial roles appear in several family stories. Being white, or, in some cases, native born, allowed greater privileges for the white parent. As the white parent was frequently the mother, traditional gender roles could be reversed in the process. Issues of race and facility with language contributed to power differences between parents. Mary Ignacio described how this affected her parents and led her to identify with her father: "I didn't identify with him because of race, but I did identify with him during arguments my parents would have. I mean, I felt for him. Whenever there was an argument, my mother was definitely more facile with the language than my dad was. And so my dad just couldn't keep up his end, but even if I wasn't in the room, I would try to speak for him or tell him the words in my head, the words he should be using."

Are We Family?

Disbelief in familial relationships by others, denial, and even abandonment haunt the stories of some of the people I interviewed. Sometimes there was no contact between a white parent and mixed child because of the stigma associated with the relationship. Brian Mitchell, born in 1939 in a small western town to an unmarried white mother and a black father with Native American ancestry, never had a relationship with his white mother. To protect his mother's reputation, Brian's race at birth was listed as "white." His father left town, and when Brian was an infant, he was given to a local black family to raise. Although he grew up living less than a mile from his biological mother, Brian said, "she never acknowledged me—she never claimed, or nothing was ever said, that she was my mother. And still hasn't today."

Brian's biological mother eventually married a white man and had two children. Brian actually would go to their house and play with them after school. When I asked if they knew that Brian was related to them, he said, "The answer is, words were said but there were always denials. They do now. But you know, at that point, there was nothing."

Of all the people I interviewed, Brian dwells the most on the senselessness of what being considered black has done to him. He could never comprehend why he had to be treated so differently. As he was more white than anything else, it never made sense to him. Because of his white ancestry, the insanity of the racial rules was quite apparent to him. Yet, he grew up in the 1940s and 1950s in a town with signs on the streets reading, "No niggers, Indians, or dogs allowed." There was no choice for him. His story is full of disruptions of natural feeling and connectedness because of race, beginning with his relationship with his mother. He expresses a profound sense of dissonance between his ascribed identity as a black man and how he feels internally.

The story of June Cross and her mother resonates with the denial of biological connection between white mother and child found in Brian's account. June Cross produced the documentary *Secret Daughter* for *Frontline* about her life, with particular focus on her relationship with her mother, and later wrote a book of the same title (J. Cross 2006). As a young child born to a white mother and black father, June was left with a black family to be raised in Atlantic City while her mother pursued her acting career. June's mother eventually moved to California and married a TV star. When June visited the family in California, the fiction was maintained that she was an adopted daughter. Her mother justified denying her relationship to her daughter on the grounds that she was protecting the career of June's stepfather.

Louise Soriano, born in 1931 to a Filipino father and white mother, spoke of an episode in which her mother also denied her relationship to her children, but in her case it was a matter of necessity. This occurred in rural Nebraska when Louise's mother and her family returned to the United States from the Philippines after World War II. Every time Louise's mother thought she had found housing or a job, she would be turned down when her family of half-Filipino children was discovered. She eventually came up with an innovative solution. "Eventually, what my mother did, which I thought was very smart, my youngest sister didn't think so because she was too young to understand it. Mother lied about us kids. She said she was a missionary in the Philippines and adopted us. To get housing."

Race could cause tensions within the family too. Louise's brother immersed himself in the Filipino community because of the anger he felt toward whites about the family's poor treatment. Louise recalled a conflict between her brother and mother involving race: "He called my mother a white bitch once. She said, 'Come here,' and he came, and she stood on a chair and—I'd never seen her strike anybody. And I was glad. 'Cause somehow I understood, it's not Mom's fault. You know. It's outside.... She was anguished most of the time." The accounts of these families show the extent to which racism could disrupt and disfigure bonds in multiracial families.

I also think of an issue that came up when I was doing the interviews for this book. I had a difficult time finding mixed African Americans born before the 1940s to interview. I was referred to Helen Wilson, born in 1931 and the oldest of the mixed African Americans I interviewed, by her daughter Tonya, whom I had met in an adult mixed race support group. As I began the interview, Helen told me that both of her parents were mixed. I assumed that I had been unclear that one of my criteria for interview subjects was having a white parent, but I decided to proceed with the interview anyway. I later learned from Tonya that her mother's biological father (Tonya's grandfather) was white and that the person Helen had described in the interview as her father was actually her stepfather. She may have neglected to mention her biological father for various reasons. Since he was not involved in her life at all, perhaps she thought of her stepfather as her true father. Still, since she knew that mixed race was the focus of my interest, if it were only a case of a greater sense of affiliation with the father she knew, she might have mentioned her white biological father. I can't know the reason for sure, as I did not want to confront her with the information her daughter had given me.

Lise Funderburg's book of interviews with people of mixed African American/white ancestry, *Black, White, Other* (1994), may offer some insight into Helen's secrecy about her white father. Of the sixty-five people Funderburg interviewed, the stories of only two people over fifty are featured in her book. The eldest, Emma Baker (a pseudonym), a contemporary of Helen, was very reticent about having her story told to the public. Emma surmised, but was never actually told, that her father was a white man for whom her mother had worked as a young woman. But the subject of her father was never discussed. "At home, when I brought up the subject as to who my father was and where he was, it was a no-no. It was just like a dirty word, so from an early age I knew not to say anything more about my father" (Funderburg 1994, 32–33).

Emma Baker's story raises another aspect about people of mixed African American/white ancestry. The mixed African Americans I interviewed born in the 1940s and later had white mothers and black fathers. Helen Wilson and Emma Baker, born into an earlier era in the Jim Crow South, had white fathers. Although many younger people of mixed African American/white ancestry have a black father and white mother, this is a relatively recent departure from the more historically common pattern of white male sexual exploitation of black women, which dates back to the earliest days of U.S. history (Feagin 2006). White fathers were frequently not present in the lives of the mixed offspring of such liaisons, and the relationships were often not acknowledged. This represented a radical disruption of the normal bonds of family. It is a limitation that I was not able to interview more mixed African Americans in the older age group, whose circumstances of birth were commonly quite different from those of members of the younger group.

The Family That Stays Together

We have seen some of the difficulties that multiracial families faced. Some succumbed to overwhelming pressure and became divided. However, others resisted and survived. In spite of all the difficulties they encountered, the majority of the families of the people I interviewed stayed intact. My examination of these families for characteristics that may have supported their remaining together does not yield one explanatory factor. Most, but not all, were working- or middle-class and had fathers with stable employment. Some, but not all, had relationships with both sides of the family. Several of the children of such families had close relationships with their grandparents and made a point of talking about them in depth. The role of community support was also significant, particularly when family support was absent. In some cases these families were absorbed into the community of the parent of color; in others, they were brought into close-knit networks through the parents' membership in churches or political organizations.

One forum to challenge racial separation was the organized Left, which was a force in the Bay Area during the time when many of the younger interviewees were born. It provided one of the rare social settings that, at least in theory, did not frown on intermarriage and, if anything, celebrated it as an example of multiracial unity. Therefore, it is not surprising that some of the people I interviewed had parents who were active leftists. When these participants were growing up in the 1940s and 1950s, the Left was deeply committed to racial equality, with a strong emphasis on black/white working-class unity. It was presumed that working-class unity would eventually transcend race in a classic Marxist vision of the primacy of class contradictions.

The commitment to a united, multiracial working class meant that there was an ideological foundation for incorporating multiraciality within the family and that a supportive social network existed for such families. These families generally lived in multiracial communities. The fracturing of family life along racial lines seen in the families of some of my respondents was less evident for them.

These family stories show the inextricability of family history and what we might call "real" history, that is, history involving large-scale events like wars and the institution of Jim Crow laws. Frequently, there was a seamless flow in the participants' recounting of their parents' experiences, their own feelings as children, and how they felt about being multiracial in the present. We literally incorporate our parents and carry their experiences within ourselves. There is no strict dividing line between generations. This is one reason why studying older people is so meaningful: their lives also give us glimpses of the lives that came before them.

The Influence of Family Dynamics

Family influences on mixed race identity and identification have been explored extensively, though primarily in adolescents and young adults (Kich 1992; Root 2001; Rockquemore 2002; Herman 2004; Rockquemore, Lasyloffy, and Noveske 2006; Yancey and Lewis 2009; Bratter and Heard 2009). There has been an encouraging trend toward the use of large databases like the Add Health survey (Harris and Sim 2002; Cheng and Lively 2009) and the Early Childhood Longitudinal Study (Brunsma 2005) to ascertain the influence of context and parental identification on mixed race self-identification for relatively large numbers of adolescents.

Kerry Ann Rockquemore, Tracey Laszloffy, and Julia Noveske (2006) rightly emphasize the need for more research on how parental socialization influences mixed race identity. Studies of mixed race identity in the contemporary period indicate a more complex pattern of perceived identity choices, in which there has been some relaxing of structural constraints like the one-drop rule. Appearance, community norms, and peers can influence identification. In particular, multiracial families provide foundational experiences and messages about how racial difference is handled. With regard to black/white families, the parents typically have distinctly different experiences of race and racism, and their experiences and beliefs come to bear on how they raise their children. Rockquemore, Laszloffy, and Noveske divide the ways mixed parents, particularly white mothers, socialize their children around racial issues into two basic frameworks: color-blind and liberatory. In their view, black parents derive a model of racial socialization from their own experiences and from their parents that includes consciousness of inequality and skills for negotiating a sometimes hostile environment in which they are the minority. Conversely, white parents are socialized to equate race with color and frequently lack consciousness of having a race and of the privileges of being white. Since white mother/black father is the predominant contemporary parental pairing for mixed black/white offspring, and since mothers provide most racial socialization, the ideology of the parents, particularly white mothers, is very influential, especially for their mixed race daughters. Although Rockquemore, Laszloffy, and Noveske base their analysis on children and adolescents in contemporary mixed race families, I found surprising resonance with the family dynamics experienced by two mixed African American women almost fifty years ago.

In her seminal work on black feminist thought, Patricia Hill Collins (1991) asserts that knowledge is formed and transformed through ongoing collective community dialogue in the African American community. Black women in particular are embedded from childhood in a network of female kin, "othermothers," and female role models in church and community, who are the transmitters of collective wisdom. The identities of "black" and "woman" are inextricably entwined. What then is the situation of the mixed African American woman who has a white mother?

The following section includes the stories of two women of similar age, born to black fathers and white mothers, whose families coped quite differently with the challenges of living in an environment hostile to mixed race families. The first story is that of Grace Nelson, who provided much more detail about her family environment and focused particularly on the role of her relationship with her mother. The second story, that of Kim Cole, is briefer but provides important points of contrast with Grace's story. These women's relationships with their white family members and their white mothers' ways of dealing with race emerge as key factors in their ability to achieve coherence around racial identity.

"It Was Like I Was a Black White Woman"

Grace Nelson, an engaging, fair-skinned woman with rosy cheeks and long, wavy, salt-and-pepper hair, was born in 1949 to an African American father, who also had Native American ancestry, and a white mother. In appearance, she could easily pass as a person of Mediterranean or Latin ancestry. Speaking with her several times in the office where she works, I was amazed by the territory she traversed as she responded to my questions in her direct style. I also had a chance to observe her interacting with other employees in her department. During an office party, I was astonished to hear her break into song in clear, resonant tones. Like her mother, whom she describes later, in my observation she sings "black." I had the impression that the black employees in her office looked up to her as one of their own, even though, as her story suggests, she might not agree.

Throughout the interviews, Grace used the word "schizophrenia" in reference to her biracial experience. As the story of her life unfolded, her reasons for using that term became clear. Splitting of the self by race emerged as a significant theme and began a generation earlier with her mother's marriage. Grace described her parents' marriage in Nevada before that state's law against interracial marriage was overturned.

> And so what my mother did was, she dressed up as if she were a black woman. My mother is white and my father is black. And so she disguised herself as a black woman by putting brown gloves on and coffee-bean stockings. Put pancake makeup on her face and a hat on her hair, and she and my father went before the judge there to get married. And she said she was scared to death, and the judge looked at her and said, you're the strangest-looking nigger I've ever seen.

The casualness with which "nigger" could be used by a person with considerable status and authority says much about what could be taken for granted at that time. The hostile environment toward race mixing placed enormous stress on mixed race couples and families. Grace doesn't know much about her biological father, as her parents' marriage ended in divorce when she was three years old. Ironically, Grace's mother was able to have her marriage annulled by claiming it was illegal!

When she was five, Grace and her mother moved to Oakland, where her mother married another black man, who raised Grace as his daughter. By then, interracial marriage had been legalized in California, so her mother and stepfather were able to wed without subterfuge. However, legalizing unions such as theirs did not lessen the hostility toward interracial couples. In the early 1950s, Grace remembers, her family was subject of considerable scrutiny, exacerbated in her view by the fact that her stepfather was very dark, making it clear that her parents were a mixed couple. "I remember people driving down the street, almost running into trees. They would punch their spouse or their mate or whoever it was with them, like we were strange things, to be looked at." The family also received more ominous attention from the police, who stopped them constantly. Because Grace's stepfather had a Cadillac, the police assumed he was a pimp and that her mother was a prostitute. They always carried their marriage license so they could prove they were married. The effects of living in such an environment enhanced the family's sense of isolation.

Grace's mother was disowned by her family of origin—with the exception of Grace's maternal grandmother, who lived with Grace's family—and Grace grew up without knowing most of her white relatives. When I asked her how she identified, Grace credited being so cut off from the white side of her family and being seen by everyone as a black child for her never questioning her identity as black. "How else could I see myself? No matter whether I was as light as my mom or not. Somebody somewhere defined me as black early on, and that's the label that I took on, never questioning that perhaps it was different than that."

With her stepfather's side of the family, "we were just part of the family. We grew up as a black family. We lived in a black community. We were churched in a black community." Grace describes her family and mother as deeply assimilated into black life, particularly their Pentecostal religious community. As Grace said about her mother's singing, "She was a soloist, and she sang in the black church, but I grew up hearing it always, 'She does not sing like a white woman.' So it was as if they saw her white but heard her as black." Unbeknownst to Grace, her mother even dyed her hair dark brown to fit in.

Yet, Grace's mother had a completely separate white life at work. Grace discovered just how separate this life was after her mother died, when she learned that only one close work friend knew that her mother had a black husband and children. Grace's mother kept the racial identity of her family secret for fear of losing her job, which was a real risk at that time. She strictly divided her life along racial lines. When she was at work, she was completely white. When she was in her community, she lived a black life. Yet, although race was deeply embedded in how the family lived, paradoxically, it was a taboo subject in the household. As Grace said, "It was just very, very weird. My parents didn't allow you to use color. You didn't talk about white, you didn't talk about black, which seems so bizarre when you think about it, because *that's what we were all about.* I knew my mother was white, and I knew my father was black, but we didn't talk about it."

Because of their strict religious beliefs, her family life was cut off from much of the outside world except for the church, further contributing to Grace's isolation. "Very, very strict, antidrinking, antismoking, antidancing, antisocial, period. Anything that you liked you couldn't do. You understand? Nothing. Zero." While Grace initially described this environment as race neutral, as our conversation deepened, she revealed that her mother transmitted some less-than-positive attitudes about blacks, particularly those she considered "lower-class." This came up when I asked Grace what advice she would give to younger people from mixed backgrounds. In the process of answering that question, Grace described her mother's behavior as an example of what *not* to do if you have a multiracial family. She said it was important "to make sure that derogatory things are not said or done or implied." Grace spoke of her own internalized racism toward blacks, which she traces to her mother. "I had racism even against my own race that I naturally gravitate toward, and I find myself saying things, behaving in a way I have said whites do when they stereotype blacks. A lot of that came from what I heard from my mother growing up." Although Grace's mother and stepfather were together and of an earlier generation, Grace's experiences of her mother's racism resonate with those Rockquemore (2002) describes in her analysis of some of the negative messages transmitted to biracial women raised by single white mothers.

While Grace's family was totally absorbed into the black community, the prohibition on discussing race in the home had a curious effect on her. When I asked whether her sense of racial identity had been influenced by the civil rights movement, she replied, "I know this sounds crazy, but I don't remember the civil rights movement. When I say black stuff was not allowed, I don't even remember. I have friends who marched. Are you serious? We didn't get black magazines. My parents didn't have *Ebony* and *Jet* magazine. I don't know what happened to me. It's like I was asleep during the civil rights movement. It's like, I literally have years cut out of my thinking. We didn't discuss it."

Not until Grace was in her early thirties did she have "an awakening" on taking an African American history class at a local junior college. She had never read anything about black history and knew nothing about the slave trade. "I went into that class as if I were white, even though I was black. It was as if someone turned light bulbs on in my head. I had no sense of history. And I had this marvelous teacher. I must have been a strange animal to him. It was like having this black white woman in his class. And I was reading stuff, and I was like, Nat Turner? Who are these people?" The class changed Grace's life and started her on a journey of connection with her black heritage. She discovered a sense of pride in being black and became interested in African American and African art, which she incorporates into creating ceramics. Learning about black history also caused her to reconsider some of her long-standing assumptions about her mother. Grace remembers occasions when her mother was treated with hostility by the black women in their church. Learning about black history gave Grace some context for understanding this treatment. As she said, "My mother was clueless as to some of the things she was doing that were so offensive."

When I asked Grace about aging and racial identity, she said that she's been on a "journey of self-discovery that's not just about race but about being a woman." When I asked her about a sense of difference, she said she feels both gender and racial oppression and most uncomfortable with well-educated white men. During her twenties and thirties, she was more focused on exploring African American history and culture. More recently, however, she has become more focused on her identity as a woman and mother. A theme in Grace's life has been her search for older female mother figures.

She reflected on a difficult time when the racial contradictions of her mother's life came to a head. Her mother went through a crisis over what she had given up, which was essentially her identity as a white person. Her regrets over her choices were very painful for Grace. "It was very hard for me emotionally to hear her. She would call me when I was at work, and she would be crying. She wanted family, and she had none. She gave up everything to marry, and she ended up saying things like, 'If I had it to do over, I wouldn't have black children.' And that was very, very painful for me to hear." The most dramatic manifestation of her mother's crisis occurred when Grace was speaking in church one night. "My mother walked in, and her hair was platinum blonde. I was speechless because she'd always dyed her hair very dark brown, and that's how I knew her. She said that she wanted to go back to looking like she did when she was a child. But to me it was symbolic, and I don't know if it was her way of saying, I really am white."

After her mother died, Grace felt a strong need to connect with older white women. During this period, Grace and her husband joined a mostly white church. She explained her motivation: "I had an intense desire to be around white women who looked like my mother and who were her age. I needed that. And I got that from those folks. I get something from their nurturing, and I know it's tied up with race. It's sort of like, I go on this quest looking for a mother to kind of replace this mother that's gone. I recognized that I was actually patching together some kind of quilt of emotional support from these people who looked like my mother."

At the same time, Grace expresses a deep yearning for a greater sense of connection with black women. She feels that she missed something essential because of her lack of exposure to black women growing up. She belongs to a black women's writing group, which functions more like a support group for her. "They provide for me some sense of connectedness to the black heritage of my family. The only elder I had was my white grandmother. And I feel like there's this big hole, a sadness or a void that I have there. And so I love hearing the stories or being connected with families that have, like, three generations where you can see that." Even so, she acknowledges that she hasn't felt completely at home and accepted by blacks, and she feels hurt when the sense of community she seeks from black women doesn't happen. "There are places where I don't fully have a clue, or I may have a clue, but it's not all knowing, because I haven't experienced life in the same way that they have. They have black mothers, black families, totally, and there is some common ground there that I just don't know anything about."

Grace feels she has to work harder at proving she's black and is very aware of talking and moving differently, depending on which group she's with. She finds herself "speaking black" when she's in a black environment. Yet, she is conscious of this performance of race (King and DaCosta 1996), which again reinforces her sense of difference from other blacks. In spite of growing up in a black community, she often feels like an outsider, especially in church communities. Some of this she relates to her appearance. "Not only was my skin color different, my hair was different, so I didn't have what they called kinky hard hair. There's this thing in black culture, you know, good hair, black hair, bad hair, light skin versus dark skin. It's just sickening." When I asked her for an example of what barriers come up for her now, she said, "It's more what isn't said and what isn't done. Just recently I was at church. Someone commented on my hair. And I said, 'Oh, this is my gel look. I just wash it and put gel on it and go.' And it was like there was this difference with the person I was talking to.

'I can't do that with my hair.' I didn't mean it to be I'm better than anyone. But again, it's sort of, 'You're not the same as we are.'" Grace does feel accepted by white people and described her white female friends at work as a kind of "sisterhood." She's been told that she doesn't pick up on the cues that whites are being racist that her black friends see. As she said, "How can I? That was my mother. You're talking about people who were my people. My dearest person in my life was my maternal grandmother. Well, I'm sorry. I don't know how to make her, and anyone who looks like her, into ogres."

In summary, Grace feels at home with white women because they remind her of her mother. She talks like them, which sets her apart from other blacks. Yet, with regard to identity, she said, "I am black, yes. That is the dichotomy. That is the paradox." Though she frequently feels like an outsider and not quite accepted by blacks, she does not question her fundamental identity as black. "Black" has been such a powerful category in her life that it encompasses a complex subjectivity full of contradictions. These contradictions are particularly poignant for Grace because she sees the inextricability of the identities of "black" and "woman" for other black women, and she lacked guidance on how to be a black woman. She experiences being both black and white as a dichotomy. As a result, Grace doesn't feel totally at home racially anywhere.

We develop identity in complex ways, but certainly we learn an important part of what it means to be a "woman" or a "man" from our parent of the same sex. When parental role models are absent, we may turn to a grandmother, aunt, close family friend, or all of the above. With such a powerful traditional association between race and gender identity for African American women, we see in Grace's story how challenging it has been for her to develop a coherent sense of self that encompasses the whole of who she is, when the dominant female influences in her life reflected only one of her ancestries, the one that is at odds with how society has traditionally categorized people like her. Her story points out the importance of employing an intersectional perspective in research on mixed race and examining the influence of parents of different races and genders (Crenshaw 1995; Berger and Guidroz 2010).

Grace's family's way of not dealing with race seems extreme, but at the time she was growing up, other mixed race families were scarce, and there were no models for how best to nurture the children in an environment predicated on a mutually exclusive conception of race as either black or white. Grace's mother did not abandon her children like Brian Mitchell's mother did, but she split her life completely along racial lines. Although she lived a black life outside of work, paradoxically she enforced the prevalence of white values by the de facto banishment of blackness in the home. And in midlife, she regretted the price that she had to pay for having black children.

In Grace's story we see how family and community influences can be at odds. She grew up totally immersed in the black community. Her mother immersed herself in the black community. Yet, despite literally disguising herself, Grace's mother transmitted her own cultural values and ways of being to Grace. One cannot blame her for this; she was doing what she could in an environment in which interracial marriage was still highly stigmatized, as evidenced by her need to keep her marriage secret at work for fear of losing her job. Just as her mother's life was split along racial lines, so is Grace's sense of racial identity. She quite clearly articulates the paradox of her identity: she never questions her blackness because she simply was not presented with any other option, yet she feels most comfortable with whites.

This splitting of self can occur if both sides of the mixed race person aren't acknowledged and nurtured and if connections aren't built to both sides of the family and community. Grace's story eloquently depicts how the destructive power of racism can divide the self of the mixed person and how hard it can be to develop an integrated identity in a highly racialized world.

And yet, Grace has shown remarkable ingenuity in creating a complex support system for herself. She is highly articulate and aware of both her needs and how to meet them. She creates community for herself where she can. And she shoulders the burden that so many mixed race people do—that of bridging the gaps in racial understanding. As she said, "I can be an advocate. I constantly try to get my church (predominantly black) to remember that there are other people there, and even when you think about a church or community that's black, it's typically got other heritages mixed in. There should be sensitivity around that, so that people are included rather than excluded." She feels that her mixed heritage gives her a better understanding of difference. She is able to recognize how the things that people say affect others because "I'm on both sides of the fence, so I can see it."

Is a split racial identity inevitable for older people of black and white ancestry? In the story that follows, Kim Cole's family handles race quite differently. The way Kim conceptualizes her identity differs significantly from Grace's frequently expressed sense of racial dichotomy.

"When I Say I'm Black, That Doesn't Mean I'm Not Also a Hungarian Jew"

I interviewed Kim Cole, an animated, light-skinned woman with straight brown hair and striking green eyes, in her comfortable home. Two years younger than Grace Nelson, Kim also grew up in Oakland. Like Grace, she had a white mother and a father with both African and Native American ancestry. Her parents wed in 1943 when interracial marriage was still illegal in California. They have their own story of overcoming the odds to marry. According to Kim's brother Sam, whom I also interviewed, their parents took the train to Seattle for the ceremony, as interracial marriage had been legal in the state of Washington since 1868. When they got off the train in Portland on the way, they were surrounded by a group of hostile whites. Luckily, the black sleeping car porters managed to escort the couple back onto the train. The couple married in Washington State and returned to the Bay Area, where they worked in a variety of blue-collar jobs and raised their family. Like Grace, Kim remembers repeated police attention to her family on family outings, with the same assumption that her mother was a prostitute and her father a pimp.

However, there were some important differences in the family environments of these two women. Kim grew up in a family that embraced both heritages. Her white mother came from a Hungarian Jewish family, which had seen its own share of discrimination and persecution in a Chicago neighborhood where they were the first Jewish family. There were cross burnings on their lawn, and in 1929, when Kim's mother was six years old, she witnessed the Ku Klux Klan invading her house.

Another difference between the two families was that Kim's father's family had a strong history of intermarriage, and the stories of his white and Native American ancestors are as well known to Kim and her brothers as his African American kin. Most significantly, race was not a taboo subject in the family, and both parents were political activists committed to fighting for racial equality. Resistance in the form of an alternative ideology that welcomed multiracial unity formed the basis for Kim's family experiences as a mixed child. This was reflected in Kim's Jewish grandparents' acceptance of their black son-in-law and mixed race grandchildren. She described her childhood environment: "I was aware of the race thing by the time fifth or sixth grade came along, and the fact that there was some kind of stigma associated with being black, but we were always raised to be proud of our family. I really think that my family laid this wonderful foundation down. I don't know if it's because my grandparents were immigrants that they were very loving—those kind of rare people who are just loving. So we had a lot of self-esteem. And my mother thought I was just so beautiful. She told me that." Unlike Grace, Kim had a large, supportive extended family on both sides, as well as a community and friends that included people of different races. Some of her closest friends growing up were of mixed backgrounds.

When I asked Kim whether race was talked about in the family, she affirmed that it was, if for no other reason than that it played such a big part in their lives. Both parents had been fired from jobs when their interracial marriage was discovered, validating Grace's mother's fears.

Kim did well in school and went to a top university, where she majored in Afro-American studies and was active in the Black Student Union. When I asked her about whether she ever felt that she was treated differently, like Grace, she talked about colorism in the black community. "There's always this thing, light skin, straight hair, within that community, that's gonna cause some stuff. But it's not the majority of my experience."

As for Grace, gender is very much in the forefront for Kim. When I asked what her advice to a younger person of mixed background would be, she focused on the specific issues of young women: "Just be real aware of yourself and proud of yourself and the different parts that make yourself up, but be aware of how this country functions and how you're perceived, and how we operate. If it's a young woman, I'd also go into the woman thing. Because I think that there's not only racial oppression in this country but sexual oppression, gender-based oppression. Especially for young women, I think it's real important that they be aggressive about their sense of self." Like Grace, she feels the most different from white men, and she has good female friends from a variety of backgrounds.

Because of the prevalent attitude that one drop of African ancestry made you black, Kim thought of herself as such when growing up. However, she always felt close to the Hungarian side of the family and was also encouraged to explore her Native American ancestry. She spent a summer on an Indian reservation and felt she looked Indian and fit in there. Because she grew up in an environment that accepted all of who she was, Kim sees no contradiction between identifying as black and being mixed. In fact, she made the point (echoed by Spencer 2006) that "black" itself is a multiracial category and that virtually no African Americans have pure African ancestry: "I think of myself as a black person who's also Native American, Hungarian Jew, so I don't think of black being just one thing. I don't have two parents that strictly identified as black, but that doesn't make me less black. So when I say I'm black, that doesn't mean I'm not also a Hungarian Jew." She showed me a picture of her father's large extended family, exhibiting various manifestations of their African, Native American, and European ancestries. She also told me that there were photos of the whole family throughout the house and that a picture of her Hungarian Jewish grandparents occupied a treasured place in her bedroom. Clearly, both in reality and symbolically, this "black" family embraced a variety of colors and backgrounds. For Kim, there is no contradiction between having a white mother and her secure sense of self as a black, multiracial woman. She is able to identify comfortably as a black woman and as multiracial and multicultural because she came from a background where black and white were not experienced as mutually exclusive. There was no attempt, as in Grace's family, to deny race and its power. Paradoxically, that has given her a more expansive sense of identity and a more complex vision of what being black can be.

Grace's parents made race a taboo subject within the family, but race was still present. According to Grace, emblematic aspects of black culture like black magazines and discussions of the civil rights movement were not allowed. But the absence of black culture did not make the environment "race neutral." It only ensured that the dominant racial paradigm in the family was invisible—that is, whiteness. One difference between Grace's racial socialization and the color-blind approach (Bonilla-Silva 2003) described by Rockquemore, Lasyloffy, and Noveske (2006) is that in the contemporary framework, the color-blind approach to identity emphasizes mixed race or whiteness and de-emphasizes blackness. In Grace's time, the color bar was still so strict that this would have been impossible. The one-drop rule ruled, and you were either on one side of the line or the other. Yet, perversely, the color-blind ideology prevailed in the home where manifestations of blackness weren't allowed. So the paradox for Grace was that she was de facto black, yet her home environment effaced blackness.

Kim's family experience more closely fits the liberatory ideology described by Rockquemore, Lasyloffy, and Noveske (2006). Her family did not ignore race and racism. Perhaps most significantly, both sides of Kim's family espoused an alternative ideology to the dominant racist paradigm and were actively involved in the struggle for racial equality. The fact that Kim's white mother came from a Jewish immigrant family also meant that she had experienced membership in a targeted group. Whiteness in the context of Kim's mother's family was not associated with invisibility or feeling like a part of the majority.

Grace and Kim have a lot in common. Both of their families withstood repeated harassment and discrimination. Both women stressed how important gender issues had become to them and emphasized their resonance for mixed race African American women in particular. But while Grace articulated a sense of loss for not having major African American female role models, Kim never expressed such sentiments. On the contrary, she spoke with palpable fondness of her white mother and grandparents and of what a fine foundation they provided her for developing self-esteem. While Grace and Kim described many similar experiences, such as how light skin and straight hair are viewed in the black community, the meanings they assign to these experiences are quite different, as is the degree to which they resonate at the core level of identity. Their stories suggest that even though older mixed race people of prior generations grew up in very challenging times, having a split sense of identity was not inevitable, and the way families dealt with race was a crucial factor in racial identity formation.

Note

1. According to Evelyn Nakano Glenn, Japanese immigrant women in Hawaii were the exception to this gendered pattern of immigration. Allowed

to immigrate as spouses after the 1907 Gentleman's Agreement restricted immigration of Japanese workers, Japanese women in Hawaii labored in the cane fields, albeit at lower wages than their male counterparts (Glenn 2002, 197).

3

Mixed Race Identity

The Racial Chimera

The Racial Chimera

As I scrutinized the transcripts of the interviews upon which this book is based and searched for a unifying framework to explain the everyday experiences of mixed race people, just when it seemed that I could say something coherent and conclusive, the landscape would shift. I would notice something new in an interview or something in my own personal experience as a mixed race person that just didn't seem to fit with how others had conceptualized mixed race identity.

In my struggles with this material, I became entranced by the metaphor of the chimera. I had understood this word as referring to something illusive and shifting, which surely described my experiences doing this research. Upon further exploration, I found that the word "chimera" derives from a mythological Greek creature—a monstrous hybrid with a lion's head and body, a goat's head arising out of its midsection, and a tail ending in a serpent's head. The word can be used to describe any imaginary monster with incongruous parts. Curiously, it is also used in genetics to refer to an organism whose cells come from genetically different sources. This combination of illusion and hybridity provided me with a metaphorical point of departure for conceptualizing mixed race identity. Here are some meanings of chimera and their relevance to mixed race identity.

Chimera—an illusion or fabrication of the mind

Race is a chimera, an illusion, a fabrication. Belief in this fabrication has been integral to the rise of an economic system that justified extreme exploitation. It is monstrous because, although an illusion, it wields immense power. It has radically influenced the circumstances of millions of people and, indeed, has meant the difference between life and death for some.

Chimera—an individual, organ, or part consisting of tissues of diverse genetic constitution

If race is a chimera, mixed race is doubly so. Mixed race people represent the illusion of race multiplied by two. Like this definition, a mixed race person is presumed to be a kind of collage of diverse genetic parts patched together from the fabricated "racial" differences of their parents according to the ideology of race.[1]

Chimera—a horrible or unreal creature of the imagination

For those who believe in the sanctity of racial boundaries, the mixed race person is indeed a horrible creature. This person's hybridity is an affront to the hierarchy of "races," constructed on the basis of inherent difference.

Chimera—a vain or idle fancy

If race is a chimera, so too is racial identity. It represents identification with an illusion. Therefore, for the mixed race person, racial identity is doubly chimerical.

An Ontology of Mixed Race Identity

The people I interviewed shared one commonalty: all have been deeply affected by the presence of race in their lives. All of them have, at some point, been seen as people of color and treated differently than they would have been had they been white. People of mixed race are no less affected by the belief in race than the unmixed; race simply affects them in ways that are perhaps more contradictory and complex. The unspoken and largely invisible framework for their discussions about the meaning of mixed race is that they take place within the context of what has historically been a white supremacist society, the legacy of the "racial dictatorship" (Omi and Winant 1994), and the ideology of race. By white supremacy, I'm not referring primarily to active, organized white racists, although certain of the people I interviewed or their parents had faced encounters with such groups. I refer to living in a country in which greater privileges for whites have been legally sanctioned for most of the nation's recorded history. According to Michael Omi and Howard Winant, the United States has been a racial dictatorship for most of its history. They outline three consequences of the racial dictatorship, each of which is particularly salient to the position of mixed race people: the definition of "American" identity as white, the sharp demarcation of whiteness from nonwhiteness by the color line, and the combining of different groups into "races." To these consequences, I add the beliefs that race is real and biological and that there is a natural hierarchy of races, which together comprise what I call the ideology of race (Tashiro 2005). Mixed race people challenge, and are challenged by, all the foundational components of the ideology of race.

Equally important is the effect this structural inequality has had on subjectivity. Part of the privileging of whiteness has been its invisibility with the unspoken assumption of whiteness as the norm and the marking of racialized others. The very practice of categorizing by race, which plagues mixed race people, originated in white supremacist ideology, with its belief in innate and essential differences between unequal "races."

Within this context, racial identity has some perplexing characteristics. Rather than being defined by who one is, race and racial identity are typically defined by who one is not. Not everyone has a "racial" identity. Those who do are those who are not-white. More accurately, until the recent growth of whiteness studies in the academy, only the not-white have been racialized. By using the term *racialized,* I emphasize that becoming "raced" is a sociological process, not a biologically determined fact. We are all born with a given set of physical features and genetic characteristics. It remains for the social environment we live in to racialize those characteristics, to organize our appearance and ancestry into a "race." In a society that still considers whiteness the norm, a not-white, or racialized, identity is problematic because it departs from that norm. Those who are racialized are the visible carriers of "race," while that which defines the boundaries of the racialized (i.e., whiteness) remains invisible as race. This has been born out empirically in research that has shown an astounding lack of awareness on the part of whites of the degree to which race has shaped their lives (Frankenberg 1993; Bonilla-Silva 2003; Feagin and O'Brien 2003). It is also confirmed by the way the people I interviewed described the circumstances under which they felt more white, which essentially included those times when they didn't have to think about race. This may very well be changing for younger generations, particularly in localities where whites are just one of many minority populations and where people of color have some degree of political power. However, when the people I interviewed were growing up, the powerful were white, and whiteness was considered the norm.

If the absence of race (i.e., whiteness) is the norm, then the very presence of race is problematic. Racial identity belongs to those who are raced. When you interject the concept of mixed race identity into the problematics of racial identity, the whole construct becomes even more unwieldy. Each of the people I interviewed was mixed between a white parent (not racialized) and a parent who was racialized. This type of racially mixed person embodies a supposed dichotomy. Half of the racialized/not-racialized dichotomy is visible and stigmatized (Goffman 1963); the other half is invisible. If race is constructed relationally through the binary opposites of whiteness and color (Hall 1997), then the mixed race person, in a sense, has no race. Mixed race people don't fit into the racial hierarchy. They embody an unresolvable dichotomy that is not balanced and is weighted toward the racialized half in terms of visibility and stigma but toward whiteness in terms of power and invisibility.

If race is a chimera, so too is racial identity. The so-called mixed race person embodies all the contradictions inherent in the illusion of race. Therefore, it makes sense that racial identity for the mixed race person is particularly elusive. The notion of a stable mixed race identity is doubly contradictory and did not emerge as a distinct entity in my study. Instead, I found that the people I interviewed talked about matters of race and identity in multiple ways. In general, the more racism they'd experienced due to being identified on the side of color, the more they self-identified as belonging to that side. This especially applied to the mixed African Americans. When members of a racialized group experience intense oppression because of their race, racial identity can become an inextricable part of group identity. But even most of the African Americans experienced other aspects of identity. The chimerical nature of mixed race identity is evident in the many dimensions of identity expressed by the people I interviewed.

Dimensions of Racial Identity[2]

> I think race is a loaded word. And it's comprised of many facets. It's not necessarily just the color of your skin or biologically where you came from. It is also influenced by how you were raised culturally and how you were raised socially and what economic status you have. All that plays into it. So it feels like it's much more tangled than separate.
>
> —Grace Nelson

In keeping with Grace Nelson's thoughts, rather than a single entity of "racial identity," I found multiple dimensions pertaining to matters of race and identity for the people I interviewed. Some of these dimensions were stable, and some fluctuated based on circumstances and historical context. This variability is not surprising, given the contradictory social processes involving race that mixed race people are exposed to (Mead [1929] 1993). I organized participants' comments about race and identity into five dimensions of racial identity. These terms are widely used, and some, such as *cultural identity,* have a variety of associated meanings. More often than not, there are differences in the dimensions expressed by the same person. For the purposes of this discussion, I invoke the following meanings when using these terms:

- *Cultural identity* encompasses one's core values and ways of being in the world. It may be such a core part of one's self that its characteristics are unconscious until difference is encountered. It is influenced by family and community experiences.

- *Ascribed racial identity* refers to how one is racially identified by others.
- *Racial identification to others* refers to the way one identifies oneself to others, such as when one selects a racial group on a form.
- *Racial self-identification* refers to how one truly identifies; it is probably the closest in meaning to the term *racial identity* as it is popularly used. This dimension can include multiple identities.
- *Situational racialization of feeling* refers to one's whiteness, or Asian-ness, or blackness, based on circumstances and context.

Some of these dimensions were more meaningful to the participants, particularly cultural identity and ascribed racial identity. These differences in perceived importance are reflected in the amount of material presented for each dimension. Four dimensions of identity for each participant can be found in chart form in appendix A. Unfortunately, I was not able to fit all the responses that I categorize as situational racialization of feeling in table form simply because the responses were so varied and dependent on context. Whenever possible, I have used the terms people used to describe themselves. This necessarily results in some inconsistency of terminology; for instance, some described their white parent as Caucasian, while others described that parent by ethnic identity, such as German American. However, I feel this disadvantage is outweighed by the opportunity to convey the flavor of how people actually described their heritages.

Cultural Identity

Cultural identity encompasses one's core values and ways of being in the world. It is about who we are and what we've absorbed from the people around us: family, close friends, community. Cultural identity is core, and its development is largely unconscious. Charles Daly, a mixed Japanese American born in 1948, provided a good description of cultural identity when he talked about his "Japanese-ness," which he attributes to his close relationship with his Nisei mother: "But I've always felt that the Japanese-ness has been under the surface and has been passed on and inculcated, not really overtly, but definitely strong. More in how you are in the world."

Cultural identity can also come from close community ties and relationships. Gus Pimental described the process he went through one evening after a friend asked him about his "genesis," meaning, "Who are your people?" This happened when he was in his late twenties, on a night when his mother asked him to take her to a dance at the Filipino social hall. He arrived at the dance hall pondering the answer to his friend's question.

> When I got into the building there were all these people that hugged me and held me and called me *Ninoy* like they did when I was a kid, and *Ninoy* means in Filipino "darling little boy." There were all these friends of my father's and people I had seen all my life ... so I walked around and saw all the pictures that go all the way back to 1932 when the club was first founded, and then from 1940, all the way up into the fifties—there were pictures of me and my sisters and my brothers on this wall. Each year. Me, as a boy and on and on and on ... and really looking at all these people from these newfound eyes and sensitivity about my genesis and saying, *This is who I am. This is what I come from.*

Gus's white mother's family had essentially disowned him, his parents, and his siblings. He was raised in a multiracial neighborhood with strong ties to the local Filipino community. Culturally, he identifies as Filipino American. Gus's sense of self is affirmed by the recognition of his community and the continuity he sees displayed in the pictures of his family in the community hall. He "knows where he comes from" because he sees himself embedded in a community of Filipinos that provided a rich and nurturing social environment for him and his family when he was growing up, unlike the white side of his family, to which he had little exposure. "We never had any contact with them, so in terms of having any real contact with the white part of my background, it was never really there. And when it was there, it was a negative piece, and so subconsciously I just put it off to the side and felt to myself, and pretty much still do, in terms of when I talk about who I am, I tell people I'm Filipino, Spanish, and Scotch. I don't necessarily get into the Spanish and Scotch side. I don't know anything about it quite frankly."

However, cultural affiliation for the mixed race person can be challenged on the basis of appearance, name, language, and other factors. For example, Gus described what happened later on that evening at the Filipino social hall.

So I'm standing there, and I'm having this drink, and this dude, this Filipino guy, in that club, comes up to me, and he says something to me, and I responded to him in English. And he said, "Oh, you don't speak Visayan," see because my father's province is Visayas. Then I said, "No, I don't." He said, "Are you Filipino?" I said, "Oh yeah, I'm half Filipino." And he said, "Oh, you're a half-breed." And when he said that to me, see, you know, I used to fight people over that. 'Cause when he said it, he said it in the most derogatory way that he possibly could say it, and I looked at him, and I said to him, I said, "No, man, I'm a mestizo." ... So anyway, it was resolved that night. Stuff came to a head, but it was a very wonderful and bitter experience in terms of what I've always experienced in terms of not letting anybody try and pigeonhole me, in terms of being half this or half that.

This experience was particularly poignant and memorable for Gus because of its contrast to what he had been feeling just before about being a part of the Filipino community. His story illustrates a recurrent theme in mixed race life of challenges to one's authenticity, to one's right to claim an identity of color.

Even if one looks the part, these challenges can be based on an absence of authentic cultural attributes. The lack of exposure to a community can contribute to a lack of cultural identification with it, resulting in dissonance between how one is perceived racially and one's cultural identity. This dissonance seemed to be more pronounced for the mixed African Americans who participated in my study. For example, Brian Mitchell was raised by an adoptive black family, but in a rural area with very few black people. He described his sense of not being accepted by black people based on the lack of traits he associates with black culture: "They ran into a problem with my style and my way of talking and walking and lack of knowledge of how to be black—I just never lived in a black environment at all. So I was almost too white, or too straight, or I didn't know the words to use. But to them it was apparent that I was different."

In addition to his way of talking and walking, other "obvious things" include his not dancing right, and he said he gets irritated with blacks who "shuck and jive." Although Brian can fit in with other African Americans on the basis of skin color, he feels he cannot pass culturally. He lacks the kind of intimate community connections that Gus had. There is dissonance between his ascribed black racial identity and his cultural identity. Interestingly, Brian and some of the other mixed African Americans I interviewed attributed their lack of black cultural experience to a lack of family connections to the South. There's a sense that the South is the source of "true" black culture and identity. In other parts of the interview, Brian said he identifies as black because that's the only category that's been available to him. Yet, he also said that he's more white than anything else (which is technically true, since he is only one-quarter of African descent) and that he's most familiar with a white environment. Brian doesn't feel completely accepted by either group. He said, "It was like you were in the middle there someplace, wherever that someplace was." As a result, Brian feels most comfortable in multiracial, multicultural groups. He has worked in international settings for most of his adult life and feels that his experience as an outsider in the United States has given him skills and versatility in adapting to other cultures.

People may engage in performative strategies to fit in culturally, a behavior reminiscent of the observations of sociologist Irving Goffman (1959, 1963), who envisioned the actor as consciously manipulating his or her external reflection through presentation of self to enhance self-esteem, while simultaneously becoming the creation of that reflection. Goffman's perspective on the performative aspects of the self applies to the strategies some of the people I interviewed described for "acting black." These strategies most commonly take the form of changing speech patterns based on the racial milieu, as well as employing different ways of moving the body in the "performance" of blackness, the second face of race described by King and DaCosta (1996) in their analysis of the levels at which race is socially constructed. But there remains a sense of being on the outside, on the fringes, as one participant put it. Although they are seen as racially different by whites, several of the people I interviewed also described challenges to the authenticity of their identities as black or Asian by people of color.

Ascribed Racial Identity

> Race had not been important *to* me, but it had been important *on* me, if that makes any sense.
>
> —Fred Johnson

Ascribed racial identity entails how one is racially identified by others, or the racial identity that others "put on you." We are not born with racial identity. We learn that we have a race from the people with whom we come into contact, who reflect that identity back to us. Several of the people I spoke with described their earliest memories of awareness of their racial difference. Larry Trumble, a mixed African American man who was fifty when interviewed, described his first experience of being seen as racially different at the age of six.

> Then the time that I also remember was like these people, it was kind of weird, you know how things stick in your mind, but I re-member crossing the street, and there was a family that lived across from us. We were actually kind of close to them. And one of the girls used to babysit for me.... And the brother, we were crossing the street, and it was sort of a friendly atmosphere or something, and he said something to me about that I was a Negro or colored or something. He was telling me I was really different from them. And I remember being really shocked because I didn't really think of that.... So if somebody said, "Well, your hair's different, or your skin's darker," that wouldn't have been a surprise, but the way they kind of put it, it was very violating, because I felt safe initially with the people, with my babysitter, and then that this brother would interject that, it was really, that's my first remembrance really of a racial incident.

Prior to this experience, Larry has little memory of racial awareness. He used the word "violating" repeatedly in the rest of the interview that is the source of this quote. There's a sense of race being violently imposed on him and his powerlessness to resist it. In a later part of the interview, Larry said that once he became a teenager, he experi-enced daily racist incidents in the northeastern city where he grew up. Although he continues to feel more affinity for white cultural values, for Larry, the power of ascribed identity outweighs cultural identity in terms of where he feels safest.

> I probably feel more part of white culture in certain values than I do black culture in certain values, but I always feel an affinity with black people on another level that I don't really feel for white people, just because my experience externally has been more that

of a black person and not of a white person.... Your strongest experiences are negative ones often, and where I've felt most threatened in my growing up was by white people. I never would feel if I walked into a poor black neighborhood that it would be a problem. And it never was. But it was always from white people, especially in the teenage years.

Although Larry feels more culturally white (he said this in other parts of his interviews as well), he has an affinity for black people because of the safety he feels with them. His use of the word "externally" to describe his experience as a black person magnifies the degree to which his blackness is about what shows on the outside, as contrasted with what he feels internally. Yet, the magnitude of the racism he experienced due to his apparent identity as a black man has profoundly influenced his sense of affinity.

When the externally ascribed identity is relentlessly reinforced, it can become inextricably mixed with core identity. Grace Nelson talked about this process:

> For me, it's all I've ever known. Even though I grew up with a family that was mixed racially, my identifying factor has been black. That's what it feels like. That's all I've ever known. And that in itself has foisted on me a way of seeing myself whether I want to see myself that way or not. I don't know how to separate it. It's like, those lenses are glued on. I was basically unable to defend myself from that label. They saw me, and I saw myself that way.... Their view and my view were sort of comingled in determining who I am. And no matter whether I could stand and scream and say I am just me, I don't know if that is even possible. I'm black. Someone said to me, "Well, why did you choose it?" Choose? They said, "But you're half white and half black. Why didn't you choose white?" What? There was no choice. I was raised with that notion, and I mean, that is one thing I heard from as far back as I can remember: one drop of black blood, you are black. That's it.

Grace's statement "They saw me, and I saw myself that way" is an example of the reflective social process of identity construction described by Charles Horton Cooley ([1902] 1993) in his classic "The Looking Glass Self" and by the contemporary concept of "reflected appraisal" (Khanna 2004), meaning how we think others see us. However, Grace's reflected view of herself was limited and structured by the oppressive rules of racial categorization for blacks (Omi and Winant 1994). Like Larry, she uses terms that express her sense of helplessness in the face of external imposition. Her choice of the word "defend" indicates how much this process of racialization was not of her own volition. Yet, despite the fact that this racial identity was imposed from without, it "comingled" with her view of herself. It became a part of her. Thus, the relentlessly reinforced externally ascribed identity can also become inextricably mixed with racial self-identification in a process similar to that Goffman (1963) describes for the incorporation of stigmatized identities into the self.

Each of the mixed African Americans echoed Grace's comments about "one drop of black blood." Although currently one's assigned race is based on self-identification, this is a relatively recent phenomenon. For most of our history, race has been determined by others. The legacy of Jim Crow laws, with their restrictive racial definitions, was alive in the society that Grace and the other mixed African Americans I interviewed grew up in.

In general, the mixed Asian Americans talked less about the effect of being viewed externally upon their internal sense of identity, save for those who had experienced intense racism. For example, Louise Soriano described identifying purely with her Asian side because that's how others see her: "Dutch, Irish, Welsh, Chinese, Filipino, Malayan. And of course when I look in the mirror, I'm Asian, I'm Filipino, and that's how people see me, and they wonder why I speak English.... I am Asian to the larger society, that's all there is to it." Again, in Louise's remarks, we see the interplay between externally ascribed identity and self-identification. I do not think it is coincidental that of all the Asian Americans I interviewed, Louise's experiences of racism were closest to those of the mixed African Americans. Her Filipino father had repeatedly been physically attacked by white racists, and Louise and her family experienced severe discrimination in housing, employment, and education based on race. There is a direct correlation between the extent to which people suffer racism and the degree to which they internalize their ascribed nonwhite racial identity.

Although none of the mixed African Americans mentioned having been seen as anything other than black or colored, most of the mixed Asian Americans described a wide range of identifications by others. They have been identified as Hawaiian, Mexican, Native American, Italian, sometimes by their actual Asian ethnicity, and as generic "third world," brown people of color. Although ascribed identity did influence the mixed Asian Americans to feel not-white, the lack of specificity in how they were seen in comparison to the mixed African Americans correlated with a greater sense of freedom and, in some cases, advantage. For example, several of the mixed Asian Americans mentioned the benefits of being able to fit in with different minority groups and in international settings because of the ambiguity of their looks.

In contrast, none of the mixed African Americans mentioned having been seen as anything other than black or colored in the United States. Internationally, however, they also experienced a greater range of external identification—for example, as Arab in the Netherlands and as Cuban in Cuba. Those who had these international experiences found them liberating and eye-opening. As Sam Cole said, "I've always felt, especially when I travel—I went to Latin America and then started to pick up a smattering of Spanish—I could be at home anywhere, and I wasn't always first identified as a gringo, an American. I mean, going outside this culture really validates me. And in Cuba especially, it was like, Wow, this is home. Everybody looked like me." Sam's quote touches on an advantage that many multiracial people feel they enjoy. Having some degree of phenotypic ambiguity allows them a greater range of places where they can fit in with local populations. They have this flexibility on the basis of appearance. At the same time, they may have the deeper problem of not feeling like they really fit anywhere because of problems like cultural and racial dissonance, described so clearly by Brian Mitchell, Larry Trumble, and Grace Nelson.

Racial Identification to Others

People talk about racial identification in two ways. I have divided them roughly into how they identify themselves to others and how they say they truly identify. Sometimes these are similar, sometimes not. Racial identification to others refers to how multiracial people self-identify publicly, particularly when they are confronted with forms that ask them to choose a race (these interviews were conducted before the 2000 census change allowing self-identification with more than one race). For all of the mixed African Americans, this meant choosing

"black" on the forms. For the Asian Americans, there was more variation. Some would choose "Asian," mentioning such factors as their
appearance (not looking white) and a desire to help increase the number of Asian Americans as an act of political solidarity. Some might
choose "other," or write in a category like "Eurasian," or simply check
multiple boxes. Most expressed frustration at not feeling represented
by any of the standard choices. None of the people I interviewed would
check "white." The reason stated most often for this was that they were
not seen as white, as Charles Daly pointed out. When I asked him
how he would identify himself, he responded, "It would depend on
who was asking, and why. If it was like the forms … if it says 'Asian,'
I check 'Asian'; if it says 'Japanese,' I check 'Japanese.'" However, he
said he wouldn't self-identify as white "because white's generic, for
one thing. And also, because when a person's half anything nonwhite
and half white, they're identified as the nonwhite part. And whatever
statistics are being done, whatever the importance is to be identified
by ethnicity, I want it to be known."

However, later Charles said, "Yeah, and to tell you the truth, I
don't really feel very Asian." His remarks underscore the perils in
attributing too much meaning to the way multiracial people self-
identify on standard forms, which can involve a situational aspect.
As Charles indicates, the answer depends on who's asking, and why.
There frequently was little relationship between the act of fulfilling
a bureaucratic requirement to categorize oneself and how people
described actually *feeling* they racially identified. In that sense, though
of a different generation, Charles's approach mirrors that of many of
the mixed race adolescents described by David Harris and Jeremiah
Sim (2002), who identified themselves differently based on context.

Racial Self-Identification

This brings us to the other use of racial identification: how people say
they truly identify. Mixed African Americans said they really identified
as black, colored, people of color, third world, and mixed. The terms
they used were influenced by their generation. Helen Wilson, who
was sixty-five years old when interviewed, used the word "colored," a
term that none of the middle-aged mixed African Americans used.
There was variation in the dimensions of identity people expressed,
sometimes within the same interview. For example, Larry Trumble,

who felt white in his cultural values and had a sense of affinity for blacks because of his ascribed identity, said in terms of his actual identification, "But I see myself as third world more. 'Cause that's how I identify more than being black." Larry's quotes contain multiple aspects of identity and identification. He *identifies as* third world. He feels a sense of affinity and safety with black people because of the way he is *identified by* others, and he would identify himself to others as black. Yet, culturally, he feels more white. For Larry there is nothing that corresponds consistently with a unitary concept of racial identity.

The mixed Asian Americans self-identified as American, Asian, Filipino, Eurasian, people of color, third world, both, and neither, and in some cases, they did not feel they had a racial identity. Among this group, there were more people who felt that race or ethnicity was not prominent in their daily lives and that other aspects of identity were more important for them. Like Larry, many also expressed identifying in contradictory ways within the same interview.

Situational Racialization of Feeling

People often mentioned feeling more one side of their heritage or the other. The conditions that produce episodic shifts in how one feels racially can involve both similarity and difference. For example, although none identified as white, several described the conditions under which they felt "more white." Their descriptions of these moments resonate with the notion posited in the literature on whiteness that white identity is experienced as a lack of consciousness of race. The times of feeling more white are experienced as the absence of race and the absence of feeling different. Whiteness is not actually experienced as a separate racial identity; it equals not having to think about race and being able to go about your business. As Charles Daly said, one of the privileges of being mixed is that you can sometimes forget about race, particularly when you are focused on another role. For example, when asked what kind of situations make him feel more white, he responded, "Well, one is, I think, when I'm not very aware of race. I tend to feel white, which to me, on some kind of level, is just like nothing. ... When there's another role, another identity that's more prominent and visible and at the fore, then I tend to feel that. ... I get to be who I am without having a racial slant on it." Mary Ignacio portrayed feeling white as the absence of feeling different: "I think

I feel white all the time, in a way. Unless the situation makes me feel uncomfortable because I look different."

Grace Nelson talked about feeling more white when she is alone than when she is with her darker-skinned husband and children. This came out in a long exchange that was difficult for Grace, so I'll provide the full text, beginning with her response to my question about circumstances in which she feels more white.

CT: Do you ever feel or see yourself as more one side or the other (black or white), and if so, under what circumstances?

Grace: It's because I think that some things I've done without ever thinking about it consciously. What you're doing at first when you think about—some stuff that I do unconsciously. I probably see myself—although I would never label it as that—more in touch with being white—this is so weird to even say this 'cause I say I'm not, but when I'm alone and I'm out, like if I'm out shopping, or if I'm out in a restaurant, or if I'm out in the world alone, and it's not in, say, predominantly black areas or a black environment, I think that then I'm less conscious of being black.

CT: That raises an interesting question, which is, Does "less conscious of being black" equal white?

Grace: I don't know. That's why I say I don't know how to label it. It's hard to talk about this, it's so weird. Or maybe it's the flip side. Maybe I see myself through whites' eyes thinking that people don't necessarily know what I am, and so—I can't describe what it is, but I know something happens, but I've never had to actually think about it, to talk about it.

CT: Is it that you feel you're more anonymous, maybe, in a situation like that, where people don't know who you are?

Grace: Could be. This is really weird. This is trippy. I've never really—haven't talked about it. I'm distinctly different. I know that I'm different when I'm with my husband and I'm out. There's a different way internally even how I carry myself. And how I'm viewed.... I mean, when I shop, and I'm alone, I feel less—like if I don't have my kids with me, or if I'm not with my husband, I don't feel like I'm suspicious. It's that ridiculous, but it's sort of like, I can go in, and I'm a lot more relaxed. I'm not worried about people thinking that I'm gonna shoplift or take something or that I'm going to be a less credible buyer. And I'm gonna be treated differently.

More freedom is associated with the experience of whiteness—the freedom to shop without surveillance and not to feel different, not to stand out. One partial privilege enjoyed by some mixed race people is the ability to occasionally escape the oppressiveness of racialization and feel the freedom of whiteness.

   Those people whose white parent had a strong ethnic affiliation, however, did not view whiteness as the absence of racial identity. Sam Cole, whose mother was a Hungarian Jew, described himself as a "wannabe black Jew." To Sam, feeling more Jewish does not reflect an absence of culture or identity. At the same time, he says he never feels white. He distinguishes a Jewish identity from a white one. He feels a sense of positive identification with being Jewish because of the richness of the cultural exposure he had to his loving Jewish immigrant grandparents, described in chapter 2 by his sister Kim, who lived with his family when he was growing up. Because most of the Jewish side of his family was killed in the Holocaust, Sam grew up with intimate knowledge of Jews as a racialized oppressed group, like blacks. Since his whole family, both Jewish and black, consisted of political activists, he also understood the history of resistance to oppression in both cultures. When I asked him what kinds of things made him feel his Jewish identity more, he said, "What makes me Jewish? I love the ritual, the antiquity of it, the years on the calendar, the mystery of it, not only the Torah but the other books that I've always wanted to study and never had a chance to. I love to hear the prayers in Hebrew. I think they're beautiful. I really do, I just love it." As he's gotten older, Sam feels an urge to go back and study Judaism, even though his early experiences with organized Judaism, described in chapter 6, were not positive.

   Despite his strong identification as a black man, Sam is disturbed by anti-Semitism in the black community. He feels his difference when he is around other black people who make anti-Semitic comments. He understands the long history of black and Jewish alliances in progressive causes like the civil rights movement; however, given his feelings about black anti-Semitism, he makes some interesting remarks about what makes him feel black: "And that particular kind of warmth brothers feel for each other that have been through stuff together, that we've been taught to share again by Minister Farrakhan. In his own way he's brought a whole bunch more brothers together than has ever been before.... I think the Million Man March was an epiphany for a lot of black men. It really made me proud to be a black man, and know that my sons were." Sam feels his blackness through his sense of belonging with other black men and describes himself as black in this passage. The fact that Sam both identifies as a Jew and praises Louis Farrakhan could seem quite contradictory, as Farrakhan is known for his public anti-Semitic remarks. Yet, it is not a contradiction to Sam. Perhaps it is only a contradiction if viewed from the perspective that you can be either black or Jewish, but not both. Time and again, the people I interviewed displayed viewpoints that seemed contradictory, but only if identity is conceptualized as singular and exclusive. If a defining characteristic of mixed race subjectivity emerges in these interviews, it is the ability to transcend dichotomies effortlessly.

At times, mixed Asian Americans also feel more like people of color. In a typical scenario, someone will make a racially offensive remark, perhaps even about another ethnic group. Charles Daly described his internal reaction when this happens while he is with a group of white people:

> And when the topic of conversation comes around to something that has to do with ethnicity, then I feel it more acutely. And depending on who I'm with. Also, there's times where, if there's, like the mix at work is, there's now three black people out of eleven, but for a long time there was only one, that was a psychiatrist. But now there's three, and in the lunch room, sometimes I really feel either in the middle or aligned with them, when somebody says something that's like, has racial overtones and I don't even know that it does, I feel myself shift over to their side of the room.... And so it depends on the company, and what's going on. And I feel kind of chameleonlike sometimes.

Although he says he feels like a chameleon, the experience of difference prompts Charles to "shift." He describes that shift as almost subliminal. When one of his white coworkers says something racially offensive, even if Charles is not consciously aware of it at the time, he feels a shift within himself toward the black coworkers sitting at another table. He is chameleonlike in terms of his changeability but not in terms of blending with those around him. In fact, it is in relation to them that he feels his difference, his color.

People may speak of situational identification in episodic terms. Todd Sasaki, first quoted in the introduction to this book, gave two examples in this regard that arose in the context of war. The first was in response to my question about early memories of feeling different. He talked about feeling his Japanese side: "There is one thing where I realized I was different. I was different because my grandmother was in Hiroshima.... Everybody was cheering that we'd dropped the bomb and the war was over, and I remember not being happy and not cheering and realizing that my grandmother was in Hiroshima." Yet, Todd also recalled feeling Jewish during the time of another war: "A lot of it has to do with how you perceive things, and I remember during, when Israel was attacked in the Six Day War, all of a sudden I was ready to go to Israel." Todd's comments highlight the tendency to feel a given side of oneself when it is under attack and, hence, to experience a heightened sense of difference. The events Todd described occurred under the extreme circumstances of war, but such shifts can be as subtle as those Charles experienced, in which merely being "nonwhite" caused him to empathize with his black coworkers when the white group engaged in racial remarks. In general, the mixed Asian Americans were more likely to feel white—or, more accurately, not to think about race—than the mixed African Americans.

Notes

1. This is reminiscent of early "scientific" beliefs about the perils of race crossing, such as those of Charles Davenport, the first American geneticist to focus on human genetics, who published a paper in which he warned of the dangers of cross-breeding between two different races because combining the different characteristics would lead to disharmonious results in the offspring (Provine 1986). For example, crossing a tall race with a short one would yield children with either large frames and small internal organs or vice versa.

2. Portions of this section were previously published in Tashiro (2002).

4

Axes of Difference

Race and Intersections of Class and Gender

Although a small number of people were interviewed, certain patterns of difference emerged. The first involves the ages of the participants. In general, there is less variability in how the people who were around sixty-five and older when interviewed expressed their views of themselves racially. There is also more consistency in how they view themselves racially, understand their cultural identities, and identify themselves to others. Self-identification as "American" is also more prominent among this group. Chapter 6 provides an analysis of these age differences. In this chapter I discuss the influence of race, class, and gender on mixed race identity.

Differences by Race

As observed in the previous chapter, the mixed African Americans have experienced greater consistency in ascribed racial identity than the mixed Asian Americans. Although the labels may have changed from "colored" to "black" to "African American," the mixed race people of African ancestry still overwhelmingly feel that they are identified by others on the basis of that ancestry alone, whereas the mixed Asian Americans have experienced more variety in external identification. This difference in consistency is also apparent in the ways that the two groups identify themselves to others. Again, the members of the mixed African American group primarily identify themselves to others as black or colored. Thus, ascribed racial identity is consistent with how these individuals identify themselves to others. Most have also incorporated a black or colored identity into racial self-identification. The mixed Asian American group shows more variability in how members identify themselves to others. In addition, there is less correspondence between how they identify themselves *to* others and how they are identified *by* others (ascribed racial identity) than for the mixed African American group.

In the process of analyzing the interviews, I compiled a list of the factors influencing identity and identification that mixed African and Asian Americans mentioned in the interviews. The two groups shared many of the same factors, like "how you look," "social class," "the situation," "community." However, I noted that the mixed African American list was about two-thirds the length of that for the mixed Asian Americans. The differences between the lists offer insights into the differences described in dimensions of racial identity between the two groups. The Asian Americans described factors missing from the African American list, like "the language you learned," "your last name," "international experiences," and "accent," reflecting the association of Asian American identity with markers of foreignness. This is not surprising, given that some of the people in this group were immigrants, and the U.S.-born participants were, at most, only three generations removed from the country of origin of the Asian parent. None of the mixed African Americans were this close generationally to immigrant status. However, additional factors on the Asian American list include "who your friends are," "whom you relate to," and "what you do," which are also absent from the African American list. Conversely, in the African American group, two factors are absent for the Asian Americans: "lack of choice" and "skin color." From the totality of the responses of both groups, I believe that these two items, particularly "lack of choice," explain the relative paucity of factors influencing African American identity. This variation reflects the differences in the racisms experienced by African and Asian Americans.

Referring back to our original framework, racial identity is constructed through interaction within the context of social structure and relations of power. Part of that structure has been the historic privileging of whiteness and the racialization of people of color. This has taken the form of discriminatory laws and practices. As pointed out in chapter 1, there have been both commonalties and differences in the treatment of African and Asian Americans in the United States. The most restrictive racial definitions have been applied to African Americans through the rule of hypodescent, or the one-drop rule, which defined anyone with any degree of African ancestry as black. And anyone defined as black was subjected to discrimination and exclusion in every aspect of life.

Mixed Asian Americans have not experienced as much systematic definition by race as mixed African Americans. While individual court cases deemed mixed Asian Americans not-white, there was no legal codification of racial definitions defining the status of mixed Asian Americans comparable to that applied to mixed African Americans. Discrimination against Asian Americans has aimed at reinforcing their "foreignness" by restricting their immigration and access to citizenship. The association of Asian Americans with foreignness and un-American-ness persists.

Mixed African Americans expressed lack of choice consistently in the interviews, particularly in relationship to ascribed identity. There is a relentlessness to being constantly made aware that one is seen as black. There is nothing comparable for the mixed Asian Americans, who are seen in a variety of ways. Consequently, the mixed Asian Americans seem less imprisoned by racial definitions. Their remarks indicate a greater element of volition, a greater play in the ways they are able to identify. Therefore, situational factors, like friends and occupations, can have greater influence on their identities.

Because of the history of the one-drop rule, the experiences of mixed African Americans with regard to confronting racism are closer to those of African Americans who do not consider themselves mixed than is the case for the mixed Asian Americans in relation to their nonmixed counterparts. The mixed African Americans are always seen as black, like their nonmixed counterparts. The mixed Asian Americans may be seen in a variety of ways, based on factors like appearance, name, and accent.

There is a great deal of flexibility in the dimensions of mixed race identity, as demonstrated in the preceding chapter. However, certain deep structural factors permeate the social relations of mixed people, influencing and limiting the ways they see themselves. In this case, the history of racial classification of multiracial blacks as black and black only shapes mixed African American identity. If it were simply a matter of one classification among equally valued racial groups, this racial definition would be of limited significance. But for centuries, being black meant being relegated to the bottom of the racial hierarchy, facing discrimination and racism in every aspect of life. Exclusion from white society meant that African Americans developed a group solidarity built on racial identity. This solidarity continues to influence people of mixed African American heritage. The black community has historically embraced people of a variety of ancestries. As Helen Wilson said of when she was growing up, "And I think people understood then why people in the black race were so many different colors, that there had to be a mixture, and they accepted it." In Helen's time, in Jim Crow Texas, there "had to be a mixture" because there was no choice, unless the mixed African American could pass into the white population. Even though the mixed person might have experienced "some stuff" (as Kim Cole put it) around light skin and straight hair in the black community, he or she could be accepted as part of the "black race." While the mixed African Americans I interviewed experienced a variety of different dimensions of identity, they had an affinity to being black that, for the most part, was not duplicated in the mixed Asian American group. According to what they told me, that affinity comprised a complex mix of lack of choice, loyalty, safety, shared history, and the common experience of the pain of racism. The mixed Asian Americans in my study, by and large, did not experience a comparable shared group identity with other Asian Americans.

Intersections of Class, Gender, and Mixed Race

To add further complexity to the picture of mixed race identity, I want to highlight some examples of how gender and class interact with mixed race for the people I interviewed. Race, class, and gender overlap and intersect in ways that are not merely additive (Crenshaw 1995; Hill Collins 2004) but also mutually constitutive of each other (Omi and Winant 1994; Anthias and Yuval-Davis 1992; Ferber 1998). Several examples of this interaction call to mind Stuart Hall's (1997) concept of "racialized regimes of representation." Drawing on Saussurian linguistic theory, which links the overt with underlying structures of meaning, Hall applies the concept of representation to race. Frequently, racialized regimes of representation invoke messages about gender, class, and sexuality and their intersections with race. Such representations of race can do the work of perpetuating ideology in powerful and unconscious ways. A regime of representation links underlying meanings and stereotypes in ways that may be absorbed unconsciously. Some of the racialized regimes of representation that I discuss in this chapter include the association of mixed/black men with sexuality that must be controlled, of the feminine with Asian cultural attributes, and of being working-class with nonwhite race.

White Fears of Black Male Sexuality

The intersection of race and gender was particularly significant for some of the mixed African American men I interviewed, especially around the issue of sexuality. An extensive literature examines the extreme Western/white fascination with black sexuality (Mercer 1994), particularly the role that fear of black male sexuality plays in violent white racism (Fanon 1967; Gilman 1985; Zack 1995; Ferber 1998; Hill Collins 2004). The experiences of some of the mixed African American men, who described encountering white anxiety when they got to dating age, add complexity to this issue. They spontaneously recounted very overt messages about staying away from white females. I encountered nothing comparable in virulence for the mixed African American women or the mixed Asian Americans of either sex.

Because of how the black race has been constructed in the United States, it's difficult to know for certain the degree to which this anxiety was attributable to these men's being seen as mixed versus black. But it had a serious impact on their lives, particularly for those who grew up in locations without a sizable black population. For example, Brian Mitchell, who was raised in a small western town, described his life there as pretty normal, except when it came to dating. He spoke of being part of a group of young people: "But I mean, we ran around together, I don't mean to say, there was nothing that excluded anybody. It's just, you know, was, the one thing you didn't do was have anything to do with women. Anything else you could do." When I asked him how he learned this rule about white women, he said, "It's natural, you're a little kid and you want to date and so forth, and ask somebody out. 'No, I can't go out with you. My father said you're a nigger.' And then, or I would ask somebody out, and my mother would hear about it. My mother would then tell me, you can't do that because you will get run out of town if you mess around this way. And it was true, we would." Brian made repeated references to the social deprivation this caused him and the long-term impact it had. "I could go anyplace and do anything. I just couldn't be with somebody. One of the manifestations of that was that for many, many years I was unaware of the fact that, publicly, I would not show that I was with someone, if I was in a mixed couple. Public displays of intimacy, just no, absolutely not. I wouldn't walk down the street holding her hand, I wouldn't give a kiss. There was always this sort of pulling away. Subconscious. Until the person whom I was married to said, 'Why won't you ever show any affection?'"

Fred Johnson, Brian Mitchell's half brother, who grew up in the Pacific Northwest and a rural western area that also had few blacks, described a similar phenomenon:

> I didn't have any trouble, in certain ways, fitting in, even though it was a—certain kind of acceptance, but it was not total. And as I look back, I think one of the biggest factors was girls. The more the boy/girl thing started happening, the more tension there was. And I liked girls from way back, from way back I liked the little girls, you see. 'Cause I remember in fourth grade, I tried to kiss this girl. Because I watched this stuff on TV, I tried to kiss this girl in the cloakroom. She told the teacher. And the teacher told me, she said, "Fred, you shouldn't do that. You'd better be careful, because girls will get you in trouble." And at the time I took her literally. But looking back, I think she wanted to say, "White girls will get you into trouble." ... And it's funny, I don't think I ever initiated a kiss with a woman, a girl, a female, until I was probably in my twenties. I mean, it really imprinted in my mind ... not being able to ask on dates and stuff the girls I had crushes on and stuff was one of the most painful parts of my adolescence.

The presence of a mixed black man and the possibility of miscegenation seemed particularly threatening to racist whites when participants in my study were growing up. Perhaps the light-skinned black man is a potential threat because he is closer to white and thus needs more reminders about the racial rules. As a person on the boundaries of the color line, he threatens the ideology of separate, unequal races. This was particularly true when these mixed African American men were coming of age at the end of the Jim Crow era. A mixed race black man is doubly threatening to white supremacist ideology. He simultaneously represents dilution of the purity of whiteness, a "mongrelization" as it were (Ferber 1998), and embodies imagined rapacious black male sexuality. He must be reminded of the one-drop rule that makes him black and the corresponding social distance from whites. In Fred and Brian's descriptions of their experiences, that social distance was elastic when it came to friendships with white males but rigid with regard to white females.

Gregory Williams (1996) describes similar prohibitions in his autobiography *Life on the Color Line*. Williams is very light skinned and looks white. Indeed, he is probably at most one-quarter "black," as his "black" father, who passed as white until Williams was in late child-hood, was himself biracial. Williams's account of his life as a "black" child conveys the obsessive quality of his white teachers' anxieties about his dating choices. The very fact that he looked white seemed to contribute to the vigilance with which his teachers pursued his instruction in the racial rules. To add to his dilemma, he was also harassed on the street when with black women by people who thought he was white!

The gendered response to these mixed African American men had a profound effect on their interactions with the opposite sex. In some cases, like Brian's, the effects were lifelong. There is a poignancy to his questioning about why he was considered different.

> What the issue for me was, and I remember as a child really say-ing, you know, I'm not any different. I don't talk different, I don't walk different. The only difference is the color of my skin, but I'm also more white than I am anything else. Why? And I could never—that question obviously was never an answerable question, and one of the down sides was, that's a question you didn't ask because you just didn't. You didn't question the authority, you didn't question whether it was—the fairness of being labeled one or the other. I mean, I was black. Then it was colored or Negro, or

pejoratively nigger, but not many people would call me a nigger
but they would talk about it.

Regarding his racial identity, Fred Johnson did the math and came up
with an unanswerable conundrum. Like Brian, he kept silent about
his question. "I remember when I was young, asking a question. A
lot of people think questions are sometimes challenges. And it was
a question, period; I didn't understand. I said, Well, why, if I'm half
white—at that time I thought I was half white, three-eighths black,
and one-eighth Indian—how come I'm black? It was a question: how
come? Because it didn't fit my math. But it was a question I only
asked myself. I never asked an individual." Though Sam Cole consistently identifies as black, he also asked why, albeit in a somewhat
indirect fashion, almost as if he felt the question was unworthy and
might reflect disloyalty to the African American community. "Well,
I think that people, particularly people here, people in the minority
community, people that grow up with the kind of subliminal kind of
identity issues that people like me might have, not that I didn't ever
identify with the African American community, but just wonder why,
just growing up wondering why."

Of all the people I interviewed, the mixed African American
men described encountering the most overt racism. In addition to
recounting painful experiences around dating, they talked about
being constantly subjected to racial taunts in their youth, blatant
discrimination in educational settings (tracking), police harassment,
and physical aggression. Complicating matters, we cannot attribute
these incidents solely to their being mixed. Because of the way race
is defined, these men were, and are, seen by society as black. While
the experiences of the mixed African American men and women
share commonalities, there are differences in the way race and gender
oppression intermingled for them. It would be a mistake to assume
that race and gender oppression are simply additive, without taking
into account the intricacies of how these oppressions interact. In
this small study, we see examples of how the intersection of black
race with masculinity seemed deeply threatening to whites, and history is full of the horrifying punishments dealt to black men for any
presumed interest in white women. The criminalization of young
black men may be the latest manifestation of the hypersurveillance
of black masculinity.

The Significance of Class

As I went through the biographies of the people in my study and tried to assign them a class status, I encountered difficulties. I found myself needing to consider type of work (blue- versus white-collar), income, poverty level, property and business ownership, education, and, perhaps most important, how their families were positioned in relationship to the people around them. Like race, class is experienced relationally. An occupational status deemed "working-class" can still distinguish a family favorably from those around them when others are in lower-status occupations or unemployed. I found most interesting how aspects of racial identity were seemingly influenced by class and how my respondents associated class with race. The ways they conceptualized class, like race, also varied. In the words of the people I interviewed, class status can refer to being poor, being better educated, having a better job, owning property, how you talk, and so forth. All of these aspects of class were discussed in relationship to racial identity. These markers of class recall Pierre Bourdieu's concept of the field of power, which includes the categories of economic capital, social capital (including valued relations with others), cultural capital (primarily consisting of legitimate knowledge), and symbolic capital (prestige and social honor) (Bourdieu 1977; Bourdieu and Wacquant 1992; Jenkins 1992).

Take for example Larry Trumble, who grew up in a mostly white working-class neighborhood in a northeastern city. His black father worked as a machinist, which Larry said was considered a good job in his neighborhood. The family lived in a house owned by Larry's white grandmother. Larry stressed that home ownership in particular gave his family higher status in a neighborhood mostly made up of renters. Larry said he feels more white in his cultural values because he identifies "black culture" with "lower-class culture." He is an educated professional who was raised mostly by his white mother and grandmother. He doesn't "speak black." He associates authentic black identity with lower-class culture.

Grace Nelson had a similar perspective on the association of class and racial identity. If you recall, her white mother raised her not to do certain things that might get her labeled as "lower-class black." Grace talked about how her daughter, who is not particularly light skinned, is still accused of "speaking white" by her friends. Part of the challenge to Grace's daughter's authenticity stems from her being raised in a middle-class household and exposed to experiences like travel, which are foreign to her friends.

The intersection of class with race in Grace's story involves two generations. Her story demonstrates something about the intergenerational transfer of advantage (Conley 1999). Like Larry's, Grace's family had it a little bit better than most of their community. In Grace's case, it was because her mother worked in business as well as because she enforced certain rules about speech and behavior. "I grew up with my mother, who worked in business, which during that time there weren't a lot of black women and men who were actually working in business, and my mother was pretty careful about how we spoke and the way we dressed. She had a lot of rules around that. And so I don't know if our speech kind of also separated us in a way, besides the color and all of that." As the end result of Grace's upbringing, she feels comfortable with whites, which she thinks sets her apart from other blacks. This discussion of the advantages conferred by white parents shows the complexity of how that advantage is transmitted, sometimes across generations. A body of literature has examined the effect of skin color on status and health for African Americans (Williamson 1995; Dressler 1991; Herring, Keith, and Horton 2004; Sweet et al. 2007). The comments of the people I interviewed suggest that the advantages experienced by lighter-skinned blacks may be as much about inheritance of Bourdieu's four types of capital as skin color. The economic and social advantages of white ancestry, such as owning property, enjoying higher socioeconomic status, learning white values and speech, and prioritizing higher education, may be at least as significant as actual skin color for mixed African Americans. Yet, advantages in the white world can be disadvantages in the black world, as Grace's daughter's experience suggests. One's authenticity and "real blackness" can be challenged based on speech, values, and level of comfort relative to whites. This can contribute to a sense of not completely belonging in either world, of difference based on race in the white world and culture and class in the black world.

Perceptions of race were related to class for the mixed Asian American group also. For example, Mary Ignacio talked about how she felt different in her mostly white working-class neighborhood in San Francisco. "There were a lot of things other than race. I mean, the race thing was part of it. But my mother was college educated, we lived in a working-class neighborhood, she was considered the neighborhood's encyclopedia.... And we were—it was expected that we would go to college, and I don't think anybody in the neighborhood went to college." Mary's mother's college education gave the family status in the community and meant that she had higher expectations for her children than was typical for the neighborhood. There were also differences in status between Mary's mother and father. Mary's mother was a registered nurse, and her Filipino father worked in the hospital kitchen. They met when her father was waiting on the nurses' tables. They formed a mixed-class family in which the parents had unequal levels of social and cultural capital. Mary's father worked in a variety of manual-labor jobs and had little education. This resulted in a shifting of traditional relationships within the family, a theme that appeared in the family stories of several of the people I interviewed, as previously described in chapter 2.

Class can also influence with whom we affiliate, and a shared class status can help transcend racial differences. Gus Pimental, who strongly identifies as working-class, talked about how class influenced his life and choice of friends. His Filipino father was a culinary worker struggling to support his wife and six children in San Francisco, and the family was very poor. After being evicted from their apartment when he was about ten years old, Gus's family went to live with a relative of his mother in an all-white neighborhood. He talked about his experiences in the school there and his friendship with kids from a poor white family:

> And they were poor, poor, poor, like we were. And we related to each other as a poor white family, a poor Filipino family.... And it wasn't clear to me why at the time, but now I look back at it. 'Cause we were both in the same bag. We were both comin' from the same place, man. I mean, people used to poke fun at them 'cause they were poor, and they'd poke fun at us 'cause we were poor and brown.... And it always left with me a feeling about white folks in terms of understanding some class things.... Race, that's just a goddam term, man. But class is real. Class is a real, real thing.

Although Gus says he went through a period of hating most white people, clearly he distinguished some white people from others, and his feelings about whites were not solely about color. Just as color is associated with lower class, whiteness is associated with economic privilege. Class and race co-construct each other, and, perhaps for whites too, lower class confers a kind of "color." This brings to mind a discussion by Joel Williamson (1995) concerning the height of white hysteria about "hidden blackness" in the post-Reconstruction South, when white people demonstrating behavioral traits associated with blacks were deemed suspect. Clearly, race is about much more than color, and its representation can be evoked by class and gender markers.

Intersections of Race, Class, and Gender in the Assignment of Identity

Differing class identities can influence perceptions of racial identity even within the same family. Charles and Joseph Daly are mixed Japanese American brothers. At the time I interviewed them, Charles was working as a counselor and hoped to get his master's degree. Joseph was working as a warehouseman. Although they grew up in the same working-class family and in the same neighborhoods, their age difference meant that they had different experiences. Charles sees Joseph as more "third world" because of his working-class identification. Joseph attended a multiracial junior high school, while Charles attended a mostly white junior high. Although they went to the same high school, the two-year difference in the times they attended coincided with a huge cultural shift. Charles said,

> And we went to the same high school, and he [Joseph] didn't fit in there, and I fit in fine. And I think it was cultural. He identified with—most of his friends were Caucasian, but at the same time, he identified more with working-class values. And I was—by the time I finished high school, it was 1966, and that stuff was brewing. When he was in high school, the people that smoked pot were the hoods. When I was in high school, the people that smoked pot were the artists and the hippies. And the hoods. So I think the timing, even those two and a half, three years' difference, accounts for some of our different values, our ways of looking at race.

Charles associates class, culture, and pot smoking with Joseph's being more "third world," meaning a person of color. Joseph confirms some of Charles's perceptions. Although Joseph doesn't think much about race and in his youth identified more with white "rebels" like James Dean, his rebellious, working-class identity translated into a life that puts him into more intimate contact with people of color. His girlfriend is Mexican American, and, if anything, he thinks of himself as "brown." Yet, of his parents, he identifies most strongly with his working-class Irish father because of his verboseness and propensity for drinking.

At the same time, Charles, who says he feels more white than Joseph because most of his friends and girlfriends have been white and he has a less working-class orientation, believes that he is more Japanese than his brother. Charles associates the qualities he shares with his Nisei mother—being more quiet, sensitive, receptive, and responsible—with being more culturally Japanese than his brother. He is aware that these traits are gendered: "And I think I have a more fully developed or open feminine side than my brother." Charles admits that the traits he associates with Japanese or Asian culture have an element of the imaginary about them and may be influenced by popular stereotypes. "I have this kind of fantasy idea of what it's like to be Japanese."

The comments of these brothers indicate how class, gender, culture, and personality traits can become racialized in the assignment of racial identity. These factors all intersect in popular representations of race. Racially mixed individuals, like all people, absorb popular conceptions about what race means. For example, the association of feminine qualities with Asian-ness and the resultant demasculinizing of Asian American men have been a periodic topic of discussion in the Asian American community (Mura 1996). Yen Le Espiritu (1997) attributes this construction to the history of Asian immigration, in which Asian American men were forced into feminized jobs, like domestic service and laundry work, which had gone unfilled because of the absence of women. Yet, this gendered construction has a dualistic quality. Early depictions of Asian men portrayed them as lascivious sexual predators who posed a danger to white women (Takaki 1989). Thus, the nuances of racial imagery can change with historical context and dominant interests.

On a gendered spectrum of popular stereotypes, Asian-ness is more female, whereas brown-ness and working-class culture are masculinized. In the case of these two brothers, the gendered construction of their racial identities is accentuated by their "likeness" to their raced and gendered parents. So Joseph, who thinks he's more like his father, is more "third world" and working-class. Charles, who is like his mother, is more Asian, white, and middle-class. Interestingly, within this construction there is a switch in the actual racial associations with the parents. Although Charles feels he is more like his Japanese American mother, he also thinks he's more white than Joseph. Joseph identifies most with his white father, but the masculine qualities of working-class behavior override the actual color of that identification, and he identifies more as a "brown" person. Class deepens "color" for Asian Americans as well as African Americans in the case of Charles and Joseph.

5

Eurasian or Bangus?

Other Nations and Mixed Race

Several of the older mixed Asian American women I interviewed were first-generation immigrants to the United States and had spent significant portions of their lives in Asia. Their responses to the interview questions provide insights into the status and treatment of multiracial Asians in Asian countries as well as a basis for comparison with their counterparts' treatment the United States. Their stories illustrate the global aspect of the construction of race and the lingering impact of colonialism on racial hierarchies.

Chapter 1 discusses how conditions in the country of origin and its state relations with our government influenced the treatment of Asians in the United States. Focusing solely on the United States obscures the degree to which Western powers, including the United States, have been heavily involved in Asia for centuries. Beginning in the late 1800s, I first briefly discuss the case of China, where three of the women who participated in this study grew up.

The nineteenth century witnessed a rapid escalation of Western penetration of China. This accelerated further after China's defeat in the Sino-Japanese war of 1894, which left it vulnerable and weak. In the aftermath of China's defeat by the Japanese, the United States, various European powers, and Japan carved China up into spheres of influence through which they could increase their financial domination and economic exploitation (Chesneaux, Bastid, and Bergere 1976). Foreign hegemony continued through most of the first half of the twentieth century in China.

Noted author Han Suyin, herself a Eurasian who grew up in China and has written several autobiographical volumes chronicling its tumultuous history in the twentieth century, describes China in 1919 as

> a semicolony, everyone's prey, no one's responsibility. In India, the British at least *had* to keep things running; but in China no such duty existed, and all who could swooped upon her, to grow fat and wealthy upon her carrion misery. There were all kinds of extraterritorial rights and privileges for foreigners; within her territory spheres of influence, spheres of special interest, war zones, leased territories, treaty ports, concessions, settlements, quartered her independence and despoiled her of authority. The foreigners maintained their own law courts and post offices. Even the Chinese who had lawsuits with foreign residents were subject to foreign courts; there were any number of special privileges granted to the Great Powers in respect of commercial and industrial rights, railways and mines, loans, and currency. (Han [1966] 1985, 46–47)

With such a large European presence in China, a mixed Eurasian population developed. Janet Chiang, at ninety-four, was the oldest such person I interviewed and resided in a nursing home in San Francisco. Born in Shanghai, Janet was seventeen years old during the time described by Han Suyin. Her father, a Danish customs worker, was introduced to Janet's Cantonese mother by mutual friends in Shanghai. Janet described having had a comfortable upbringing in a household with a cook and servants. She gave the impression that this was a commonplace arrangement for people who would be considered middle-class by U.S. standards. She grew up speaking English in the home and went to English school. When I asked her how she thought of herself, she said, "Eurasian. Because we were speaking English at home. My father never spoke Chinese. And my mother spoke English."

When I asked Janet whether her sense of identification had ever changed during her life, or if she'd ever identified with solely one side or the other of her heritage, she said, "No, because I was brought up Western style." Interestingly, for Janet, "Eurasian" correlates with "Western." But given the conditions in China when she was growing up, that's not surprising. During that time, portions of China had been carved into interest zones assigned to various Western powers. As there was considerable social contact between Europeans and Chinese in these enclaves, there was a significant number of offspring of mixed liaisons. The term *Eurasian* was applied to these mixed descendants and is commonly used throughout Asia for people of mixed European and Asian descent. Eurasians like Janet lived in vastly superior conditions compared to the masses of Chinese peasants. In some areas of Asia, like the city-state of Singapore, members of Eurasian communities have intermarried for several generations and occupy a distinct stratum in the social hierarchy.

Being middle-class and Eurasian did not, however, protect Janet entirely from the stigma of being part Chinese in a colonial environment. She described Shanghai as having been a particularly bad place for Eurasians. As she said, "The English girls used to—you know, they would tell us that their own people married Asiatics instead of their own." Janet was more comfortable when her family moved to Tientsin, which she felt was more accepting of Eurasians due to the residents' higher level of education and the smaller size of the city. Generally, Janet denied that race was a problem for her, which she attributed to her Western upbringing and good command of English.

When I went to the nursing home to visit Janet, I met her good friend Caroline Lowe, who also considered herself Eurasian. Caroline's mother was from Alsace-Lorraine, and her father was Chinese. She and Janet met in Shanghai when Caroline was in her teens, and the two have remained friends since then despite their age difference (Caroline was sixty-nine when interviewed). The younger woman was much more outspoken about the difficulties Eurasians faced in Asia: "I was born in Suchow, but I was raised in Shanghai. The difference I felt at that time, I think I was more accepted by the Chinese. I hate to say that. Though they used to have names for people who were Eurasians. But I was more accepted by them, but not so much by the French, though my mother was French and had a French passport. I have a feeling she was resented, because why did she marry a Chinese instead of her own?" She explained prejudice against Eurasians as having a class-based component: "They don't realize that in some cases, like my father was a very educated man. I mean, he went to

France to study, and he was an engineer. And then you had the low-class people that would marry others, but we were classified under the same. You are a Eurasian, and you cannot be any good. So you were really not accepted by one side or the other. But in my own opinion, because I had two half brothers, I was more accepted by the Chinese. And not so much by the Caucasians." Caroline returned to the issue of her mother's marrying non-French, as well as to her own status as not-white. "Well, they didn't say it in words, not like, you know, but we were underneath everybody else because we were not white. See, the Chinese made no difference, because their idea, and as a kid I remember they said that all the Eurasians are so cute looking, you know, the babies are so cute looking. But when you came to the French now, because my mother was French, when she would go to the consulate, for instance, they wouldn't even ask her to sit down. It's like, why did you marry a Chinese man?"

Like Janet, Caroline received a Western education in Shanghai. She went to a school in which French was spoken, and she learned English there as well. Caroline came to the United States with her family in 1964. She denies ever having problems in America because of her race but says that in Hong Kong it was particularly hard for Eurasians. She attributed this to the British: "Somehow the English, they are very cold by nature, that's my way of thinking.... The English definitely do not like the Chinese or the Eurasians. They felt we were not good enough." She went on to describe being passed over for a government job in Hong Kong in favor of an English girl who was less qualified, which she felt reflected prejudice against her as a Eurasian.

Although most of what Caroline describes took place in China, beliefs about white superiority influenced attitudes toward Eurasians on the part of both the Chinese and the Europeans. The Chinese thought the Eurasians were "cute looking" because this was a time when the West dominated China, bringing its ideology of white superiority. Thus, to the Chinese, Eurasians were "better" because they were part white. On the other hand, Caroline experienced discrimination by the English because she was part Chinese, which made her inferior to whites.

Caroline described her life in the United States as centered on work and family. When I asked if she remembered being affected by the various social movements of the 1960s and 1970s, particularly the Asian movement, she said she hadn't understood what was going on and was basically uninvolved. When asked to indicate her race on forms here, she puts Asian "because I don't know what goes to define Asian. It covers everything, it seems." Like Janet, she considers herself a Eurasian who has accepted both her Chinese and European ancestries.

Alicia Pereira also came from Hong Kong to the United States in 1964. She thinks both of her parents were of mixed ancestry but is uncertain about her mother, who died when Alicia was very young. As far as she knows, her father was mixed Portuguese and Filipino, and her mother was Portuguese and Italian with possibly "some Asian blood." When interviewed at age sixty, Alicia was the youngest of the women who came from China. She was still working at the time I interviewed her, which exposed her to situations in which she had to choose a racial classification. Her narrative illustrates the difference between the racial norms of Hong Kong and the United States. Like Janet and Caroline, Alicia grew up in an environment where the primary language was not Chinese. When I asked her if Chinese was her first language, she seemed irritated and said, "No, English. Like I say, Hong Kong is a British colony. . . . When I was there, the Chinese would speak Chinese, the non-Chinese, anybody of let's say white blood or mixed blood or whatever, they would speak English. That's what I did."

Alicia had clear memories of her early experiences with race in the United States. When she first came, she mostly noticed the conflicts between blacks and whites. She also got questions about her own heritage that seemed really strange to her. She remembers being asked if she was "from the islands": "So in Hong Kong, when you say, are you from the islands, it means Hong Kong island. . . . Now, when they asked me, since I was new here, I didn't realize it, I was kind of shocked. I was wondering how they knew that. Then I realized; I said, 'Oh, wait a minute. They meant Hawaii.' I guess it was because I had long hair, whatever, and I look mixed. I know there's a lot of mixed people in Hawaii. I noticed that the people here are kind of racial minded. They sort of divide people into races." Alicia says that when people find out she's from Hong Kong, they assume she's Chinese, which annoys her. She also gets mistaken for Filipino and for Hispanic because of her Portuguese surname. When I asked her how she thinks of herself, she said, "I think I look what I am. But of course, because I know what I am and I look at myself, because when I look at myself, I say, you definitely don't look white like those white people; they've got a long nose, big eyes, you don't. But then you don't look Chinese either, because you look at your complexion, you're kind of pinkish, your eyes are light, and your hair a little brown. So I like to be called Eurasian, but the trouble is, whenever I fill out a form, there's nothing about Eurasian or whatever."

Alicia talked a lot about the dilemmas of the U.S. racial categories and how she doesn't fit when situations come up in which people are organized by race. Though raised as Portuguese in Hong Kong, she can't claim that identity in the United States, because to people here she looks Asian, and Portuguese isn't considered a race. The "racial mindedness," as she put it, of the United States is clearly a problem for her because she has more of a cultural identification as Portuguese than a racial identification as Asian. As she said, "I wasn't raised as an Asian, so if I put it down, I don't feel comfortable." Her lack of cultural affinity with other Asians came through as she described an incident at work in which people were to be organized into discussion groups by race. "They were going to divide people, white, black, and Asian. So I was wondering, where on earth are they going to put me? . . . How can I consider myself Asian? Plus, the way I behave, I don't behave the way they do. They're so quiet, say nothing. I got a big mouth. So I can't consider myself Asian." For Alicia, questions about racial iden- tification were interpreted and explained in a variety of behavioral ways. The U.S. concept of race as biology didn't enter her discourse.

When I asked her whether there was anyone in her family who had influenced the way she thought of herself racially, she said,

> Well, when I was married to my ex-husband, like I say, he spoke Portuguese, so it was easier for him to tell people I was Portu- guese because he spoke the language. You see, for me, I can't tell people I'm Portuguese because I don't speak the language. So it was easier for him to have a race, but for me, I don't have a race. Like in Hong Kong, I would follow the English customs. Like I say, Hong Kong is British, here I would follow the American customs. So I don't really have customs of my own. Like people keep asking me, "What customs do you follow?" I say, "I follow the customs of the country I'm in."

This passage reflects how Alicia thinks of herself racially in terms of language and nationality, not biological inheritance. Her husband "had a race" because he spoke Portuguese. She attributes her lack of friends to her lack of a "race" because people group themselves according to race, and she doesn't really fit into any of the established categories in a behavioral sense. Of all the racial groups, she feels she's more accepted by whites, based on her behavior, although she says her preference is for mixed groups. "Like I say, I don't behave like an Asian, I don't behave like a Hispanic. I guess I behave more like a white person because I behave very independently."

More than Janet and Caroline, Alicia seems to be in transition between her country of origin and the United States in terms of her attitudes and perceptions about race. "Okay, when I first came to this country, I felt more comfortable with the Asian people, because when I was in Hong Kong, the majority of the people were Asian, so I felt more comfortable talking to them. But now that I've been here so long, and usually I notice that the men who like me happen to be white, so I sort of—I don't know, I feel I'm going more to the white side, probably because they accept me more than the Asian people. The Asian people stick to themselves more." Whereas she felt more affinity for Asians when she came to the United States, she now feels more affinity for whites because she perceives a cultural difference between herself and other Asians. As she said previously, she tends to adopt the customs of the country she's in. In this case, it seems that means white. She was not raised culturally as Asian even though she grew up in Hong Kong. The points of difference with other Asian women, such as "not speaking up," have to do with the fact that, like Janet, culturally she sees herself as Western, not Asian.

Although she has been here the least amount of time of the three women, Alicia seems to have the most conflict about and day-to-day experience with having to choose a "race." She is the youngest of the three women from China and the only one who was still working when interviewed. Many of the anecdotes she shared in which she experienced conflict around racial identification occurred at work.

Alicia expressed the difficulties of being mixed more than Caroline and Janet. She talked quite a bit about it. She doesn't have many friends, which she attributes to "not having a race" to group herself by. She also mentions a variety of factors that influence her sense of identification by herself and others. They include how you behave (she doesn't act like Asians; she's more assertive and behaves more like a white person), who accepts you (she feels more accepted by whites than Asians as a divorced woman), your early environment (she spoke English at home and was "raised as Portuguese," not as an Asian), and the "race" of the person you're married to. Her notion of what constitutes "race" has less to do with color than behavior, affiliation, and language. The way Alicia maps the concept of race does not fit with the U.S. model, and because of our "racial mindedness," she feels alienated and caught between worlds.

Louise Soriano's Story

Some of my participant's lives were so rich in the array of their experiences that their stories demand to be told as a whole. Louise Soriano, a retired educator of mixed Filipino and white ancestry born in 1931, is one such person. Her story covers life in two countries and the experience of living in the midst of war. It begins in Nebraska, moves to the Philippines, and eventually culminates in California.

Louise's parents first met at the University of Nebraska at a tea for foreign students. Her Filipino father was a University of Nebraska student, and Louise's mother was working as a volunteer at the tea. Louise didn't say much about their courtship, but we do know that her parents left Nebraska and went to Illinois in order to marry. Although both of Louise's parents were well educated as teachers, racism and deprivation plagued them and their family in the United States. Finding housing was difficult, and Louise's father was subjected to racially motivated physical attacks in both Nebraska and Chicago. The family finally found housing on Chicago's South Side in a black neighborhood. Eventually, however, the violence he had faced and his limited opportunities in the United States compelled Louise's father to take the family back to the Philippines.

Life in the Philippines for Louise and her family could be divided into two periods: before and after the war. Because her account of this period is so vivid, I provide below her story of life in the Philippines up to her family's return to the United States in 1945. War, brutality, starvation, and generosity from unexpected sources all enter into her narrative.

Life in the Philippines

"And when I was an infant, they decided to finally leave the country. My father said he couldn't deal with the violence here. He said, when it's in my own language, I can deal with it. Life in the Philippines I divide between pre–World War II and World War II. Prewar we were okay—I was the oldest girl, so I had responsibilities, but that's expected for being a good older sister. We used the honorifics for older brothers and sisters. And we were five, and the youngest was nine and a half, ten years younger than I am.

"I was treated differently in school because I came from a mixed family. There's a rhyme in the Philippines. *Bangus*, that means half-breed milkfish. The milkfish is very white meat. Dark on the inside, white on the outside. Your mother was cheap. They're referring to the Spanish-American War, where the only women who consorted with American GIs were prostitutes. So your mother was cheap, your father had a bald head, because that's what American men were known by. I guess Filipino men are bald-less! I put up with that rhyme, no matter what school I went to.

"And then I had a fight in first grade, a good fist fight because somebody was teasing me and calling my mother cheap. And then they said I could not have been born in the United States, and that annoyed the hell out of me. So I don't know who struck whom first, but I remember the fight. And then because I spoke English already—I spoke English, Ilocano, Tagalog, a number of languages—my teachers treated me differently in school. I was accelerated, for one thing. And the teachers gave me extra tutoring in math.

"The classes were in English, and for some reason, I was one of the culprits who would speak Tagalog or Ilocano, depending on which region I was in. It was punished on the school grounds, and somebody would rat on me for speaking father's language. You'd have to kneel. By the beach, it was in the sand. In other places I remember those tiny little mung beans. You had to kneel on that, or I remember my hands being slapped with a sharp-edged ruler. Even though the teachers were Filipino, they were educated by the Americans, and it was a rule in school. Other people in Manila told me they used to fine people, but that wouldn't work in the poor areas. We lived in good standard housing. My parents always tried to live close to the school where they taught.

"I never thought about being mixed in terms of my friendships. My parents objected to my friendship with a little girl in my school because her mother was a prostitute. And even then I had asthma, and I pulled an asthma fit so I could see her. I knew what I was doing. Many of my childhood friends were daughters of my mother's compatriots.

There's a Manila society of white women who had married Filipinos. So many of them were in the same situation. I remember a little girl named Betty. And there were those who teased me and those who chose me. Some of the kids thought I should have more wealth. I didn't have more wealth because my parents didn't believe in it. And then because my brothers and sisters were close together, we played together. We lived outside a lot because the weather's somewhat like Hawaii. We always had cousins, and my father had a brother in Manila who had nine kids at school. And at summertime my older brother and I went to Grandpa's farm, a little farm which was real countryside.

"During the war, we got bombed out right after Pearl Harbor. I was about ten or eleven years old. Yeah, the first trauma was the bombing. Well, really, the first trauma was, at school they put dog tags around us, and instructed us in case of an air raid we were to stay on the school grounds and follow the teacher's instructions, and there were trucks ready to evacuate us, and I came home crying. 'Cause I didn't—in case of an air raid I wanted to go home. And my parents tried to explain to me that I might not be able to go home, and the best thing would be to do what the teacher said.

"The area we lived in was destroyed, and I was—there's a servant system in the Philippines. That still remains today. And the servants started going home to the barrios because they sensed there was trouble. I was loaned out to my mother's friends who were chemists for the U.S. Navy. I happened to be right in the navy yard because I was helping Mother's friends. I had taken one of the maids that worked for us to Mother's friends, or they had taken me there, and I was the translator. Mother's friends didn't speak any of the languages. Most Americans didn't. Dumdums. Well, conquerors. So I was in the navy yard, and the house I was in was a direct hit. I got out just in time. Dr. and Mrs. M. wouldn't leave. The maid was hysterical. She was under the bed. I was a child, you know, but I ran out. My motivation—I wanted to go home. First sign of trouble, let's go home. And the house collapsed behind me in flames. And I got—I finally got home, all bloody, 'cause it was a bloody mess, and my family was under the high school where my parents were teaching. And my mother was just about hysterical because she thought I was gone.

"That evening, somehow or other, my parents got hold of a car, and I was jammed in. You know the old cars, they had a ledge in the back. I was jammed in there. It was a miserable trip out of the city, which was essentially on fire. And we holed up in a little town of No-valeta, and we dug underground air raid shelters with arched caves where we children slept. The only problem was, it was full of snakes, and the neighbors got in there and stole all the canned goods. There was a lot of hostility. My mother is blond and blue-eyed. And the hostility was now legitimate, with the Japanese occupations. There were stories, like good friends of ours who were German American, emphasis German, who actually turned out to be spies, and they headed the Japanese column coming in. That's another kid we played with. He used to pee on us.

"And so the starvation began, and that was the main fact. My father was picked up, and he looked awfully Chinese to the Japanese occupation, and he was beaten up pretty bad. The poor guy kept getting beat up, or at least that's my memory. And he soon joined the resistance movement. But the main factor of the war was starvation. Mother tried to do her bit. She joined a Methodist church group, and they smuggled clothing and lettuce and fish and whatever to the resistance movement. It's a law of physics: there's an equal and opposite reaction. The minister was Reverend Stagg and Mrs. Stagg. And we called her Mother Stagg, and there was Dr. Derby, who was a medical doctor who worked at Philippine General. I think maybe those two women, they would meet and do what they could do. And my mother joined, was part of that. I thought she was quite heroic. She insisted on tutoring Chinese students in English. There was a large population in Manila. Sometimes I used to think she was naïve; sometimes I thought she was heroic. Because all of a sudden her and my father's work was cut off. And of course it was dangerous—to go into the Chinese quarters was frowned upon by the Japanese. Finally, one of her students knocked at the door and asked her, 'Please don't come anymore.' I think she took comfort in doing that, able to support us kids. And one day she came home and was vomiting, and she had stopped, as usual, at a restaurant to have some lunch before the next tutoring, and she recognized some human parts. Yeah, Manila had come to that. And then one day there were skeletons. You know, the meat had been taken off, outside of our door.

"But what happened to Dr. Derby and Mother Stagg—two soldiers came to our door, Japanese soldiers, and they showed Mother a picture. And I was right beside Mother. And she collapsed. It was

Dr. Derby and Mother Stagg's heads, separated from their bodies. So that collapsed the Oxford group Methodist church.

"In the meantime, my brother went out trying to help. My father was gone for six months—he had gotten caught and he was in jail and he came back with one eye gone. The starvation became more and more severe, and the harassment became more and more. We lived right across from Far Eastern University, where there were troops. We children could see the horrible treatment of prisoners and of the Korean Japanese troops. We saw them as Japanese, but the way the Japanese troops treated them, they were literally slaves.

"Mother opted, and I was grateful, to stay out of the internment camp in Manila, on a red arm band, which signified enemy status. People like my mother were allowed to stay out. She felt ashamed of this. I thought it was good. She formally renounced her American citizenship, 'cause my father denied he ever had it. So she was so embarrassed over that. But she wanted, above all, to stay with us children, and they wouldn't take us into camp. So finally, when soldiers came in and ransacked the house, and my younger brother wouldn't move or bow, which we were supposed to do, my parents decided that we should evacuate to the barrio, and the other side of the coin is, there was an older Japanese community in Manila, and they had settled in the Philippines from long before. They were descendants of the Christianized Japanese of Yokohama, from the Portuguese and Spanish, and the Japanese government ended up persecuting these people, crucifying them. A group of them left, and they settled in the southern Philippines in Mindinao. And some went up north to Manila. These people disagreed with the Japanese government. Their life was in the Philippines. And there was an old man who could write, do the writing very well. He made out papers for us. He took on that job, falsifying papers, and this and that. So we probably contacted him next time we got travel papers to go to the barrio. We went north to close to where my father was from, by train and by cart.

"By the way, in Manila, the last place where we lived, our friends were two children of Japanese descent. Their mother was a widow, and she ran a store. And one morning when there was nothing to eat, I learned how to tie a rope around my waist to deaden the hunger pangs. And it was this Japanese neighbor. And she kept it covered, but she very quickly handed me some eggs. But on the other side of where we lived was the chief of intelligence. He used to climb up a ladder and peek over our wall at my mother. He wore a G-string. And Mother—it saved her a lot of times, but she's very Bible Belt Kansas, and she thought this was a shame. Father tried to impress upon her to not say anything, it's their custom. But he was a fat guy, I remember that much. Mother's indignation would rise. One morning in Manila, the postman knocked and took a letter and went upstairs. Mother was upstairs making beds, and she opened it, and then she threw her apron over her face and shrieked. We had sent our younger brother to the barrio. And she got the news that he had died. And actually he was killed by Filipinos who were pro-Japanese.

"See, there were pros and cons. In this little town, the mayor was part Japanese. We stayed with my aunt and uncle. I couldn't believe— see, the last you see of somebody they're alive. And there never was a real funeral or grave marker. There was nothing. So I kept looking for my brother and kept dreaming about him, and I'm sure my brothers and sisters did also. My uncle was willing to house us and shelter us, but my auntie was not. She was—I always think of Mother Courage. She would have sold her daughters. She really resented us being there after a while because she was a traitor, and she supplied the Japanese army. And her sister-in-law was noticed by the mayor. While we were there, the Chinese rice warehouse was burned down, including the whole family. And they had immediately befriended my mother. We stayed there from the time I was twelve until age fourteen, when we returned to the United States.

"The Japanese occupation garrison picked up my mother and father for interrogation. And I thought, I'm lost. I got terribly, terribly sick. My father said it was amoebic dysentery. I remember that, and then we proceeded to starve again. My uncle used to try and bring us food, but his wife dominated the marriage. I don't know where my father was, but we moved to a nipa house, the traditional house. A number of people came into the yard carrying torches. They were going to burn us because my mother was American and these were pro-Japanese Filipinos. And my uncle came and talked some sense into them.

"And then also, my brother was swimming, and there were these rapids. And the trick is, you hang onto this bamboo and let your legs dangle. It's a stupid game kids play. And the mayor came along with wooden shoes and stepped on my brother's hands. Yeah. And there were people who really cared and people who didn't care. My father

always told us to understand them. They were sick of the American occupation. And the Japanese slogans were, Asia for Asians. East Asia for
Asians. Nationalistic. All white men out of Asia. That got my mother.
And then there's also the enmity at that time between China and
Japan. And through the Spanish, the Filipinos, I'm afraid, had a lot
of animosity towards the Chinese. The Spanish used to persecute the
Chinese. It's like the Jewish pogroms. And the reason was, again, well,
they're heathen. The Filipinos took on Catholicism, and Protestant-
ism later under the Americans. But the Chinese had developed their
own beliefs. So there was this prejudice, I think, towards Filipinos of
Chinese descent. On the other hand, the Chinese were very useful as
suppliers to the Spanish. They were experienced traders and farmers.
At that period of history, the Filipinos were sulking and would not
supply anything. So there's all this history behind this. Well, finally,
my father joined the resistance again.

"The Japanese troops came again, and only Mother and us kids
were home, and Mother had somehow or other miraculously saved
her Bible in a mattress. You sleep on mats in the Philippines, which I
always prefer. The hard floor. The soldiers came in and broke all the
clay pots with their bayonets. And by that time I didn't have many
clothes. I had a slip and that was it. So I'm sort of hiding behind my
mother, and then they took their bayonets and slashed her mattress.
And she got outraged. I thought we were all—this is it. And she started
lecturing them. And telling them what they were doing was evil, and
so on and on. And I was amazed that they bowed to her and left. I
talked to a student from Japan, one of the well-known scholars, and
he said, 'You know, sometimes you don't believe what you remember.'
And he said, 'Now that memory is very likely true, because there's one
thing the Japanese soldier is taught to revere besides the emperor,
and that is his mother. And they will listen to an outraged mother.
So he said, 'That's probably a true memory.'

"The Americans were getting closer. News is always carried.
There's never a complete blackout. The connection was never broken.
By submarine you could get to Australia and then back to the United
States. But that was hazardous. And the main factor was finally, my
mother couldn't move. She was dying of starvation. And my youngest
sister was quite a baby, and all the efforts were towards feeding her.
And I was getting weaker. We were all getting desperate. And finally
we heard bombings. The American troops had landed not too far

away. They landed at Leyte, which was within hearing distance of Marinduque. My father was born in this province. And the bombing persevered, and the American troops came, and we were just lying there. By that time, I couldn't move. And the first influx of troops, they were an engineering crew. They were building bridges and this and that.

"And there was a Native American. The American soldiers gave us C rations, which we promptly ate and threw up. And then I don't know why he came, but he came to the house and noticed our condition. He went out—I don't know how he found it, but he found some rice, a little bit of rice, and he killed and chopped this chicken up and boiled it with ginger, which is exactly what the Filipinos would do. And first he said we could only have the broth. And then over the week he fed us more and more. Somebody asked him how he knew, since this was so Filipino, ginger, rice, chicken broth, and he said the chicken broth they used too. And he also knew Filipinos from some of his tribal group who had married into the Filipino farm-working community. But he kept feeding us until we were sitting up and then up on our feet. He saved our lives. I remember he always used to look out the window. And he kept us in food.

"The battle raged right over us. Mother was happy because she was able to send word to her mother via the army. We were getting food and getting stronger. Not that we could always digest it. The fighting increased, and my father armed me with a hand grenade. He tried to teach me to shoot a rifle, but all I did is injure my shoulder. By this time he was active again with the American troops. There was machine-gunning, and I remember the noise, the smoke, how it sounds. And my father told me, stick by your mother and brothers and sisters, and if the enemy approached, to lob the hand grenade, which I did. But I forgot to pull the pin, which was good, 'cause it wasn't the enemy. My mother said, 'You're some soldier.' Later I turned to Quakerism, to pacifism, and Mother used to say, 'I remember when you were no pacifist.'

"So they evacuated us in an army half truck and put my mother to work teaching school. We were supposed to get canned milk, but the black market got it first. My father was absent; he was in battle and used to come home once in a while, all smoky and smelly. And from Marinduque we went to Manila, which by that time was under American occupation, and we were put in Santo Tomas, which was also the internment camp, in a tent. We were still struggling with digestive problems, and it was rainy. The Red Cross was there and the army, and we used to line up for food and then upchuck half of it. I hate to think of those days.

"Anyway, our father came; he was in uniform, and he was urging Mother—as usual I was standing sort of behind/beside her—to take the first boat she could back to the United States, get medical treatment for herself and the children. He told my brother and me, 'Get an education and come back.' And his last words were, 'Clean up that country of its racism, and I might visit you.' But we were supposed to definitely—our mission was to get healthy, get an education, and go back. My mother didn't agree. They had an eternal quarrel during the war, because my father's latent nationalism came to the fore, and he became part of the resistance and he wanted to stay there. He was not—I didn't understand it then, but he was not abandoning his family. He really expected us to come back.

"When we walked around Manila from the camp, it was as flat as Tokyo was, and there were rats running all over. In our condition there was nothing else to do but to go back to the U.S. Mother then insisted that we put shoes on. We had been so long without shoes, it was very hard if you're used to barefoot walking. The Red Cross outfitted us as best it could with khakis, army stuff, and we took a military hospital ship back here. It was full of sick GIs down in the hold. The trip took thirty days because the sea was mined and they had to zigzag. We landed July 4, 1945, in San Francisco. We were up on deck ready to go. And some nuns found lice in my hair, and they pushed me into—you know those airline bathrooms? The ship's bathrooms were much better with showers. They pushed me into that shower and DDT'd me. It was effective. But I got pretty sick."

Life After War

Louise's family's problems did not end with their return to the United States. As a mixed family, they continued to face discrimination and racism. Louise's mother took the family to her hometown in Nebraska. She had problems finding work and housing because of her mixed children. As discussed in chapter 2, she had to lie about her relationship to her own children to obtain housing. The children had a difficult time adjusting to the cold climate of Nebraska and were frequently ill. Eventually, they moved to a town in the San Joaquin Valley of California. The family still faced discrimination, although at least a Filipino community in the area welcomed them. Louise remembered learning the racial rules in the town where they settled: "I very quickly learned, don't go there. Don't go there. Why? Because you're not white. You're not seen as white."

With the change in location, Louise's ascribed identity changed according to the predominant local minority group. Whereas she had been mistaken for Native American in Nebraska, in California, she was mistaken for Mexican and almost deported. "People identify you according to the minority group around. So when we came to California, then I was picked up as Mexican and being shoved onto a bus. So finally, my mother said, 'You should carry a notarized copy of your birth certificate.'"

Although Louise and her mother remained close, relations between her brother and their mother became frayed, culminating in the conflict described in chapter 2. Louise's brother was kicked out of high school and imprisoned for activity with a Mexican gang. When he got out of prison, according to Louise, "he immediately went deep into the Filipino community, and found a girlfriend and married and settled down.... And he's totally Filipino."

Louise attributes her brother's problems to two things: he missed their father more, and the war had a greater effect on him. Still, despite her allegiance to her mother, Louise identifies herself first and foremost as Asian. She said, "I always was very protective of my mother, and I recognize it fully, but I know I'm Asian. That's all there is to it. Even Mother used to say, 'Louise, you act just like your father.'" Even though she was close to her mother, Louise has a greater sense of identification as Asian because of her relationship with her father, the racism she experienced in the United States, and her life as a Filipina in the Philippines. In addition, though she was close to her mother, Louise had little positive contact with the white side of the family, save for her maternal grandmother. Most of her relatives identified her and her siblings as "little heathens from Hawaii," according to Louise. This was a marked contrast to the family's treatment in the Filipino community, which recognized both parts of her heritage and welcomed her mother.

Some of Louise's starkest encounters with racism occurred in the educational system. She was able to get a scholarship to attend nursing school, one of three nonwhite students. She described some of the misery inflicted upon her by her fellow students at a time when being in nursing school meant living and working in the hospital where the training took place: "They tormented me. And they stole my notebooks, you know, your anatomy notebooks and stuff. Because I was different. And what else did they do? They short-sheeted me. They taunted me all the time. And, oh, they made me give them the answers at exam time." In spite of all the obstacles she faced, Louise eventually found her niche in education, becoming a teacher, then a principal, and eventually getting her PhD. She married and raised a family. When I met her, she was involved in an Asian women's writing group and working on a series of stories based on her wartime experiences. In many ways, she has transcended the pain of her past, but lingering scars manifest themselves in poor health and difficulty finding culturally congruent medical care that she can trust.

Global Relations, Race, and Power

Attitudes about race are always situated within relations of power. These women's stories show the complex relationships between particular national histories and the meaning of being of mixed race. They also show that the ideology of white supremacy was brought to Asian nations through Western colonialism. This influenced the way "Eurasians" were viewed in their Asian countries of origin. The older mixed Asian women grew up at a time when Western colonialism and domination were still strong. The prejudice toward Eurasians described by the women born in China stemmed primarily from Westerners and was about their being part Chinese or, in some cases, about their representing a liaison between a Western woman and Chinese man.

The majority of the study participants had had some negative experiences associated with not being white. Several also discussed the difficulties they had encountered due to being part white. However, the messages and relations of power associated with these two types of experiences differed. When Louise was called *mestiza bangus,* or half-breed milkfish, in the Philippines, the implication was that her mother was a prostitute who had consorted with the oppressor. An inchoate sentiment of resistance underlay this taunt. Resentment of the mixed person in this context was associated with his or her presumed closeness to imperialists. This is not to deny or belittle the pain that such a taunt can cause, but it came from individuals occupying a subordinate position in the racial/national hierarchy, unlike the institutionalized oppression that Louise and her family faced for being Filipino in the United States. Here, in addition to individual acts of hostility, she and her family faced discrimination in obtaining the basic necessities of survival: housing, employment, and education. The common context for both cases is inequality and white (and Western, in the case of the Philippines) domination.

Within Asia, Japan offers an interesting contrast. Unlike China and the Philippines, Japan was able to resist Western colonialism and became an imperialist force within Asia. The Japanese government's negotiations with the United States determined the immigration of Japanese to this country (Hing 1993). Japanese immigrants to the United States were generally better educated and possessed more skills than their Chinese and Filipino counterparts.

Unlike China and the Philippines, Japan was actually a contender for world power in World War II and was an imperialist rather than a colonized nation. Wartime ideology promoted a sense of superiority over other Asian nations. Yet, because of widespread resentment of Western colonialism in Asia, the Japanese were able to effectively deploy the "Asia for Asians" argument to enlist local support against the Allies. At the same time, Louise's account of how members of the Japanese population in the Philippines aided her family underscores the peril of assuming that people make allegiances solely along lines of ancestry and nation of origin, an assumption that provided the rationale for the internment of Japanese Americans during World War II.

Since the times when these women were growing up, there have been shifts in the world balance of power. Globalization has accelerated, and one of its results has been increased migration of people in search of opportunities. This has resulted in new population dynamics, which will undoubtedly result in new patterns of intermarriage. The meaning of mixed Asian American identity will continue to evolve and be transformed by these changes.

6

Aging and Identity

The Embodiment of History

Older people carry within themselves the cumulative effects and memories of all the years of their lives (Meyerhoff 1978; Becker 1997; Luborsky 1993). Understanding something as simultaneously personal and social as mixed race identity development means understanding who people *now* were at specific moments in the *past* and situating them in the social environments they have experienced across the life span. The meaning of racial and ethnic identity is so contextual in its relationship to historical, structural matters that to talk about it outside of history and location renders any discussion incomplete and shallow.

Why should age and aging be significant to mixed race identity? To begin with, with greater age comes the chance to look back, reflect, and integrate experiences. In that looking back, we have the opportunity to juxtapose very different times with the present. We can remember the constraints of the past, pay witness to them, and, in so doing, remind younger generations that understanding the way things were yields insights into the way things are now. Race, therefore mixed race, is intertwined with changing social attitudes, and hearing the actual experiences of those who lived through the past affords the opportunity to situate mixed race in historical context. I want to clarify that by historical context, I refer not just to events and legal changes but also to social movements and changing social attitudes that oftentimes precipitated structural changes and were, in turn, influenced by them. A good example is the civil rights movement, which culminated in sweeping legislation to rectify inequality, all of which changed the meaning of being a racial minority.

There are different perspectives on the significance of historical forces in shaping the lives of older individuals. For example, in a study of sources of meaning in late life based on interviews with sixty older Americans, Sharon Kaufman (1986) observed that historical events are not essential elements of their life stories. However, Kaufman's study population was white and middle-class. These individuals had not experienced legalized second-class citizenship for themselves or their families and then seen their lives deeply influenced by such transformative events as the enactment of civil rights laws. Kaufman's work also raises the question of whether it is necessary to be conscious of the influence of history on one's life for it to be meaningful. Even though her study population was white and middle-class, I can see how the times in which they lived shaped their stories. The impact of fundamental changes in laws allowing greater opportunities for previously excluded minorities was undoubtedly less visible to those who occupied more privileged positions.

This book is replete with accounts of how history intertwined with individual lives and influenced identity. The age of the participants in my study makes the intersection of identity and historical changes visible. Three important aspects of age and aging appear throughout the stories of the people I interviewed. The first simply has to do with age itself and how far back in history the stories take us. Because I always first asked people to describe how their parents got together, their stories provide a living link to an even more distant past. The oldest person I interviewed, Janet Chiang, was born in 1902, so some of what she described in her own and her parents' lives occurred more than a century ago. Janet was born in Shanghai during a time that would be virtually unrecognizable in today's China, when European powers had carved out spheres of influence and economic concessions. Her father was a Danish customs worker; her mother was Cantonese. They were introduced to each other by another mixed couple, an Englishman and Cantonese woman. The gendered pattern of mixed marriages of Janet's parents and their friends mirrored the imbalance in national power, with the vast majority of such unions occurring between non-Chinese men and Chinese women. The world she described had its privileges, but there was also hostility toward mixed marriages and Eurasians like her, and the number of mixed families was small. She talked about the hostility shown to her by the English girls in Shanghai, who felt that Europeans should marry their own, not Asians. Reconstructing Janet's early years offers a glimpse of the nexus of racial and colonial relations in China at the beginning of the twentieth century.

The second aging-related theme that emerged concerns the importance of the individual life course and its intersection with key historical events. What was happening in the country and the world during the formative years of late adolescence and young adulthood significantly influenced the formation of attitudes about race and the spaces and discourses available to people of mixed race. The sweeping changes taking place in the United States from the mid-1960s to the early 1970s deeply influenced how many of the people I interviewed experienced being of mixed race. We are all embedded in history, though we are typically not aware of this fact. Still, some historical eras produce more profound changes than others. Likewise, in our individual lives, certain points stand out in shaping who we are today. Putting this together, I observe and discuss an important demarcation in attitudes between two age groups in this book based on their age when the changes brought about by the civil rights movement occurred.

Finally, several people revealed how their definitions of self and attitudes about aspects of their heritages changed with the process of aging. These changes did not stem entirely from an internalized reworking related to the biological and social processes of aging. On the contrary, people largely framed these transformations in the context of how social attitudes and key institutions had changed as well. A complex interactive process emerged between internal and external development.

In the next section, I discuss some basic theoretical concepts and terminology that I found useful in interpreting the age differences vis-à-vis how people described mixed race identity.

Framing Aging and Mixed Race

Our expectation that different generations will behave and think differently is so implicit we barely notice it. "Baby boom," "Gen Y,"

"Depression era" are all labels we use to distinguish various generations with distinctly different opinions and behavioral patterns. Those involved in occupations like product marketing and economic forecasting take for granted that different generations have different tastes and behaviors. Yet, generational differences have rarely been acknowledged in the mixed race literature. Since one of my core research questions was the relationship between age and racial identity for mixed race people, and the age range of the people I interviewed spanned almost fifty years, it was key to have a theoretical framework for understanding how living and growing up in different eras could shape subjectivity.

Karl Mannheim ([1928] 1997) provides one of the earliest and most insightful analyses of the concept of generation. He frames the "problem of generations" in relationship to his concept of "social location," by which "individuals who belong to the same generation, who share the same year of birth, are endowed, to that extent, with a common location in the historical dimension of the social process" (Mannheim [1928] 1997, 35). He emphasizes that exposure to the same phase of collective processes links generations, not the fact that they experience similar points in the life course at the same time. A community of location of a generation only occurs when contemporaries participate in common experiences.

Age is significant not just in terms of the chronology of the present but in relation to one's age when significant sociohistorical events occurred. Mannheim points out the importance of late adolescence/ early adulthood as the period when the younger generation begins to differentiate itself from the older. Until this point, absorption of the knowledge of the previous generation has been "aproblematical." During this period, personal experimentation and questioning become possible. Mannheim's identification of the importance of this period in the life cycle is echoed most notably by Erik Erikson's (1950) life-stage theory, which influenced early black racial identity theory (W. E. Cross 1971) and mixed race theory (Kich 1992), both of which posited an eventual resolution of racial identity. Achievement of identity is the core task of adolescence for Erikson. Combining Mannheim's theory of generation with Erikson's life-stage theory focuses our attention on what the members of each generation experienced at specific stages in their lives, particularly during the seminal stages of adolescence and early adulthood. Divided roughly into those who were born before and after the early 1930s, those interviewees at the younger end of the spectrum experienced the civil rights movement in their youth, whereas those at the older end lived under Jim Crow well into adulthood. These factors appear to have influenced the degree of complexity with which they expressed identity. This relationship between life stage and generation becomes more fully developed in the life-course perspective.

The Life-Course Perspective

Arguably the preeminent practitioner of life-course research, Glenn Elder states, "Key principles of the life course are historical time and place, the timing of lives, linked or interdependent lives, and human agency" (1998, 4). Two of the principles of the life course Elder (1995, 1998) discusses are particularly salient for framing mixed race identity for older Americans: the importance of historical time and place and the timing of lives, which refers to the developmental stage at which critical events occur. Perhaps more than is true for any other theorist of the life course, a tremendous amount of empirical evidence from longitudinal studies, starting with his landmark study of the long-term effects of the Great Depression on the lives of those who experienced it (Elder 1974), has informed Elder's perspective. He notes the particular impact of structural constraints on opportunities and how they shape individual lives.

The life-course perspective has been successfully applied as an interpretive framework for diversity in the aging experience (Stoller and Gibson 2000) and minority aging (Jackson, Chatters, and Taylor 1993). With its attention to the interaction of the individual's personal attributes; opportunity structures as shaped by such factors as race, class, and gender; membership in a particular birth cohort; and the effects of living in different sociohistorical periods, it is highly applicable to the study of aging and mixed race. There is variation in the degree to which the life-course perspective emphasizes individual development versus the impact of historical and structural factors. Glenn Elder and minority aging scholars put greater emphasis on social location and historical circumstances in their attempt to account for the diversity of aging experiences. Erikson (1950), in his seminal work on life stages, focuses almost entirely on the normative phases of the individual life, giving minimal attention to how those stages might differ or be affected by race, class, or gender. Yet, Erikson's perspective on the foundational importance of adolescence and young adulthood to the establishment of identity offers an important piece of the picture that emerges throughout many of the interviews in this book. The life-course framework is significant in that the period of adolescence and early adulthood seems most critical for basic identity formation. The events and social climate experienced by each generation in that seminal period of life are critical to the formation of identity.

It is also important to acknowledge that how meaning is attributed to specific events in a life, and when, relates to cultural norms. Adolescence is primarily acknowledged as a life stage in economically advanced nations. The life course itself is a social and cultural construct (Frank 1979; Becker 1997; Holstein and Gubrium 2000a). The cultural life course is situated in historic time (Featherstone and Hepworth 1991). That is, social and cultural views of the course of life and the resulting effects on identity can change from one era to another (Meyer 1988; Becker 1997).

Racial or Ethnic Identity, Aging, and the Life Course

Whether racial or ethnic identity persists in its importance to people throughout the life course as they age has not been well studied empirically, even for those who come from homogeneous backgrounds. Most studies have been concerned with European ethnic groups. For example, Mark Luborsky and Robert Rubinstein (1987) examined ethnicity in a study of older widowers self-identified as Irish, Italian, and Jewish. They found that the meaning of ethnicity for these men related to several factors: "First, the meaning of ethnicity in late life derives from issues of life-span development and family history. Second, ethnic identity derives meaning from the historical settings and circumstances during which key events are experienced. Third, current-day ethnic identity is situationally evoked depending on the needs and goals of individuals. Fourth, past ethnic identity and experiences continue to be reworked as raw material for current-day ethnic meaning" (Luborsky and Rubinstein 1987, 39). Luborsky and Rubinstein's research emphasizes the fluidity of the meaning of ethnicity and its relationship to life stage and historical circumstances. Though I interviewed people from a different population, all four of the above factors are relevant and came up at various points for people throughout this book. Yet, the degree of volition available to the people I spoke with was generally more limited, particularly for the mixed African Americans, than for those studied by Luborsky and Rubinstein.

To determine how mixed race identity might vary over the life course, it would be ideal to reinterview people of mixed race periodically throughout their lives. We do know that adolescent and young adult self-identification varies with context (Harris and Sim 2002; Rockquemore and Brunsma 2002), and in qualitative studies people have indicated that they identified differently in the past (Wallace 2001). A breakthrough study by Steven Hitlin, J. Scott Brown, and Glenn Elder (2006) examined self-identification by multiracial adolescent respondents to the Add Health study at two times five years apart. They found a high degree of change in racial self-identification between the two points measured. Their study adds weight to the growing consensus that, contrary to the earlier models of mixed race identity influenced by Erikson and W. E. Cross's (1971) original nigrescence model, there is no natural fixed resolution of identity for mixed race individuals. However, no systematic longitudinal studies on mixed race people exist to offer insight into whether fluctuating identity options persist throughout adulthood.

Even longitudinal studies involving "monoracial" racial identity that could potentially offer insights are quite rare. One such study is the Panel Survey of Black Americans, which has tracked a sample of African Americans over time. The first interviews for this survey were conducted between 1979 and 1980 on 2,107 randomly selected black households and included questions about a broad range of economic, social, and behavioral issues. Out of this initial group, 581 were fifty-five years of age or older. Respondents were reinterviewed at eight, nine, and twelve years after the first interviews. The data from this survey offer a window into changes that took place in the intervening years. A comparison of changes in responses to questions asked about racial identification between 1980 and 1987 indicated that the older the respondents were, the more their racial identification increased during this period (Jackson, Chatters, and Taylor 1993). In an analysis of racial group solidarity, Robert Smith and Michael Thornton (1993) point out that for black elders who came of age in a hostile and segregated environment, racial solidarity provided a source of strength, safety, and support.

James Jackson, Linda Chatters, and Robert Taylor (1993) emphasize the importance of applying the life-course perspective to the study of minority aging. In reference to the importance of different cohorts of African American elderly to the findings from the first Nationwide Conference on the Health Status of the Negro in 1967 at Howard University, they state, "The realization that today's African-American elders were the middle-aged 'Negroes' of 1967 when this report was written, starkly highlights the importance of a life span framework in interpreting and understanding the life circumstances of African Americans at every position in the life-cycle, but most importantly in older adulthood" (Jackson, Chatters, and Taylor 1993, 302).

This brings up another important point: how we talk about race changes with the times. There are different discourses of race (Hall 1997). People who are "African Americans" now were "Negroes" in 1967. The change in terminology from Negro to black or African American represents not simply a quid pro quo replacement of one term by another but entails a complex history of associated struggle. The terms *black* and *African American* could not have gained such widespread acceptance without the civil rights movement and the rise in ethnic pride and interest in ethnic roots that surged in the 1960s and early 1970s. The appropriation of the terms *black* and later *African American* resulted from changing representations of black race and increased pride in blackness and Africanness. There were profound differences between being a forty-year-old Negro in 1967 and a forty-year-old African American in 2007. People in these different age groups have experienced what it means to be black differently and at different points in their lives.

The life course can only be understood in terms of its intersection with history. The meaning of that intersection can differ according to one's racial or ethnic group membership. Today's native-born Asian American elders who were middle-aged in 1967 might have been engaged in reunifying their families in response to the 1965 amendment to the Immigration and Nationality Act. Today's baby boomer African and Asian Americans most certainly were directly affected by the Vietnam War in 1967 because they were of draft age at that time. They may have been involved in new social movements based on the affirmation of racial and ethnic identity. Thus, the historical moment, one's social location, and one's age at that moment profoundly influence the meaning attached to one's racial identity.

Those who were young adults during the period from the mid-1960s to the early 1970s, when many of the gains of the civil rights movement were being realized, speak of the profound shift these changes made in their perspectives. Real structural changes occurred in this period with great relevance for people of color. An unprecedented flurry of progressive legislation, executive decrees, and court decisions was enacted during the 1960s in response to the power of the civil rights movement. The Civil Rights Act of 1964, 1965's Executive Order 11246 instituting affirmative action, the 1965 Immigration Act, the Voting Rights Act of 1965, the 1967 *Loving v. Virginia* decision, and the Fair Housing Act of 1968 are some prime examples. People who came of age during this period talked about how critical the changes in attitudes were to how they viewed themselves as racial minorities. As Michael Omi and Howard Winant state about this period, "The black movement redefined the *meaning of racial identity,* and consequently of race *itself,* in American society" (1994, 99). The revolutionary attitude of pride in one's heritage of this period spread to other racial and ethnic minorities and deeply affected all people of color who were coming of age at that time. For example, Gus Pimental, a mixed Filipino in his fifties when I interviewed him, described the role that the Black Power movement played for him in a pivotal incident that took place in the San Francisco Fillmore District in the 1960s, when he was in his twenties.

> And I was walking up Fillmore Street one day and I saw this beautiful poster of a black man and a black woman, and they both had these wonderful Afros. And under the poster it said, "Black is Beautiful." And it just blew me away, because I grew up at a time when even using the word "black" was considered a derogatory word. So this whole period of black consciousness, because of my experience as a Filipino growing up in a black neighborhood, really, really hit me, and it hit me in terms of my own identity as a Filipino that I also was beautiful … so I would say that was one of the single-most important turning points in my life.

Where we are in our life-course trajectory, however, also shapes the impact of such dramatic changes. When Gus was having his critical experience as a young man in his twenties, Helen Wilson, a mixed African American woman also living in the Fillmore District, was in her late thirties and focused on her marriage and raising her family. Born in 1932 when the country was in the depths of the Great Depression, she grew up in segregated Texas. Thirteen years old when World War II ended, she graduated from high school in 1950. She was twenty-two years old when the *Brown v. Board of Education of Topeka* decision prohibiting segregated public education was delivered in 1954. Most of her coming-of-age years took place in the late 1940s and early 1950s. She was thirty-five years old when the last antimiscegenation laws were overturned in 1967. Thus, many of Helen's formative years were spent under Jim Crow, when the one-drop rule ruled, and there was no question about it. Not surprisingly, the context of her formative years shaped how she views being of mixed race. In her day, racial identity for people of mixed African ancestry simply was not questioned: "At that time we just identified as colored, but we knew we were mixed with these other identities. They really didn't talk too much about it. We just accepted it as a fact and that was it.... I can't understand the big hullabaloo about it." She has little patience for her daughter's fascination with her multiracial ancestry.

One of the most interesting findings of this small study was the differing complexity of the responses among those who were born before and after the early 1930s. The older cohort's responses generally seemed simpler and more matter-of-fact. They tended to be more internally consistent in the dimensions of identity discussed in chapter 3: how they viewed themselves racially, how they understood their cultural identities, and how they identified themselves to others. They expressed less situational variability in their talk about racial identity and tended not to identify themselves with pan-ethnic formations or multicultural terms like *third world* as much as the younger cohort. In general, they seemed less concerned with matters of identity. As Helen Wilson stated, "But when we were coming up, it wasn't all that questioning." More complicated and contradictory aspects of identity simply did not come up for the older group even when I tried framing the questions in multiple ways. Generally, their comments on identity were less complex and showed less range than those of the younger cohort. To put it simply, they seemed less concerned with identity.

For example, in analyzing the various ways people expressed identity, I found that Helen Wilson consistently identified herself as "colored" for the dimensions of cultural identity, ascribed identity, racial identification to others, and racial self-identification. In contrast, younger mixed African Americans tended to express more variable dimensions of identity. Part of the difference by age arises in the language of race that people used to describe themselves. For example, Helen's use of the word "colored" contrasts with the terminology employed by many of the younger mixed African Americans, such as Larry Trumble, who was born in 1946 and expressed a variety of ways of identifying: feeling culturally "white" or "not either," being identified by others as "black," identifying himself to others as "black," and truly identifying as "something else," "a minority person," and "third world." Again, this is not a case of simply replacing a term with equivalent ones. The term *third world* for a U.S.-born person of color came into common usage in the 1960s and connoted a specific relationship to a politics of solidarity with nonwhite people internationally. The term *people of color*, which I use so glibly to include all people who are not considered white, also began to be used in this context when people in radical racial/ethnic movements were finding points of unity and engaging in coalition building with each other. New pan-ethnic formations like "Asian American" came into being in this period as well.

The discourses available to us influence the ways we talk about social identities like race (Gee 1992; Holstein and Gubrium 2000b). Discourses are about much more than just language; they are attached to deeper structures of meaning and are manifestations of power or the lack of it. The language of race that is available to us organizes our experiences. For the older cohort, the possibilities were limited, as reflected by the smaller number of identities they express. Yet, the discourses of race in the present can also play a part in reworking identity for older people of mixed race. This book began with a quote from Fred Johnson relating how discovering the possibility of a mixed race identity allowed him to "stand on both feet" by enabling him to conceive of a multiracial identity. The phrase "standing on both feet" acts as more than a mere metaphor; it represents a fundamental gravitational shift in sensibility. But this shift would not have been possible without the advent of a new generation of people who explicitly identify as mixed race. And this younger mixed race generation would not have existed without the civil rights movement and the rescinding of the antimiscegenation laws.

One of the main changes affecting older and younger interviewees differently was the relative importance attached to assimilation.

The ideals of assimilation and integration as the solution to race problems were prevalent until the period described so vividly by Gus Pimental, when color became beautiful and a source of pride. This emphasis on assimilation was particularly important for older mixed Asian Americans, who were more likely to identify as "American." Perhaps this was because status as American was so hard won for them. Their experiences shaped different interpretations of the meaning of racial identity and what it meant to be a person of mixed ancestry in America. While Gus Pimental was able to celebrate his ethnic identity in his twenties, at a similar age, Jane Murakami, a mixed Japanese American eighty-one years old when interviewed, was fighting in an internment camp for the right to be treated as an American citizen. When I asked her whether she had then thought of herself as Japanese or Caucasian, Jane responded, "No, I just felt I was an American citizen. This was my country as well as theirs. That's the way I felt. Even when I went to camp, I just couldn't see how they could do that, the government." Younger mixed Asian American respondents tended to have more complicated self-identifications, such as Joseph Daly, a mixed Japanese American born in 1946, who identified himself as "rebel," "Asian," "brown," and "Irish" at various points throughout the interview.

If we look at these differences by year of birth instead of age, our attention is directed toward the significant differences between the historical periods experienced by these individuals, particularly during the times they were growing up and becoming young adults. One difference was in the degree of importance attached to identity itself. Philip Gleason ([1983] 1996) provides a useful historicizing of the evolution of the construct of identity. As he states, according to the Oxford English Dictionary, the original meaning of "identity" has to do with "remaining the same person or thing," that is, not becoming something else. Its meaning is straightforward: something either is or isn't the identity in question. According to Gleason, personal identity as we know it did not become a popular concern until it was embraced by social and behavioral scientists in the 1950s and 1960s. Gleason's analysis is relevant to the difference in level of importance and degree of complexity attached to identity by people of different age cohorts whom I interviewed.

Racial identity also became noticed and problematized. In particular, the period of the 1960s and early 1970s saw radical changes in perspective about being a person of color and the development of positive associations with a minority identity. Figure 6.1 shows some of the critical historical events in African American and Asian American history that affected the lives of the people in this book. I have superimposed the lives of six people onto a chronicle of historic events, which allows us to see how old they were when specific events occurred (see figure 6.1 at www.paradigmpublishers.com/Books/BookDetail.aspx?productID=287441).

Looking at the chart, we note that almost every event prior to 1954 is reactionary. Then, in the 1960s, a flurry of progressive legislation and agitation by social movements called for equality and claimed a positive association with color. Many of the younger participants cite this period as critical in terms of their sense of themselves as racial minorities.

These are but a few examples of why age is significant—or, perhaps more correctly, why the age we are at the time of key sociohistorical events is so meaningful for people of mixed race, as it is for all racial minorities. For people grappling with socially stigmatized identities, identity cannot be understood outside of social context, and to understand it now, we must understand it in the past. Personal identification evolves from a dialectical interaction with a host of external influences, like legal statutes, media representations, social movements, and everyday interactions.

The Process of Aging and Mixed Race Identity

I previously discussed past work on mixed race identity within the typology originated by Thornton and expanded by Kerry Rockquemore, David Brunsma, and Daniel Delgado (2009). Mixed race researchers from the variant perspective, for example, George Kitahara Kich (1992), identified a trajectory of identity stages for mixed race people, culminating in resolution. I wondered if the people I interviewed would confirm his model. When asked, most said that their sense of identity had not changed. Yet, many people talked about their racial identity in complex, contradictory, and situational ways. I came away from this research feeling that "racial identity" is an elusive entity, more aptly described by the ecological perspective articulated by Rockquemore, Brunsma, and Delgado (2009), without a natural, fixed endpoint. The responses of the people I interviewed did not fit into defined, progressive stages of identity development; rather, their comments reflected a wide range of ways they conceptualized and experienced racial identity, sometimes simultaneously.

At the same time, there are complex methodological and philosophical issues to consider when doing this kind of retrospective querying. The interpretation of past events is constructed and reconstructed through the progression of life based on new experiences, developmental changes, and changes in prevailing social norms (Rosenthal 1993; Holstein and Gubrium 2000b). When I conversed with people, I was not interested in "truth" so much as meaning, interpretation, and all the evocative richness of memory. In addition, the very act of telling their stories within the parameters of the questions I asked undoubtedly created shifts in meaning for people. In response to the rhetorical question about whether stories create life, Guy Widdershoven states, "We also, in telling these stories, change the meaning of our experiences and actions" (1993, 7). The process of telling our stories can transform their meaning to us and thus change us in the present. Some people divulged that having a conversation about their past experiences around being of mixed race yielded new insights. Experience is inchoate and unapparent until it is organized by a narrative about that experience (Widdershoven 1993). From a hermeneutic perspective, meaning doesn't exist prior to interpretation. The narrating of their life stories offers participants the potential to rework the past. Many of the people I interviewed told me that they'd never before thought about the questions I asked them. They reported that our conversations stimulated them to think more deeply about their experiences as mixed race individuals and, in some cases, to make some positive changes in their lives. Yet, by nature, these stories are unfinished as they represent one retrospective moment in a continually evolving life span.

Changes in Attitudes

When asked about aging and mixed race, several people noted changes in how they related to being of mixed heritage. Some expressed interest in connecting or reconnecting with previously unexplored aspects of their heritages.

Nancy Grant, a mixed Japanese American born in 1921 who grew up on the East Coast and in Japan, talked about how she became interested in exploring her Japanese heritage rather late in life: "Well, I still tend to identify myself more with Caucasian because most of my friends are and everything. But because I wanted to find out about my roots and everything, I'm beginning to be prouder and prouder of the part of me that's Japanese." Although she had lived in Japan for a time as a child, Nancy was brought up Western style and went to an English-language school. Her Japanese father was convinced that American ways were superior, particularly with regard to the role of women. Prior to the 1970s, Nancy's associations with being part Japanese were mostly negative, especially during World War II when she experienced a lot of fear about being singled out for being part Japanese. Like others among the older mixed Asian Americans, she sees her identity primarily as American. When I asked her what prompted her to explore her Japanese side in the 1970s, she talked about how she was influenced by the extremely popular television miniseries *Roots*, which aired in 1977. One manifestation of the rise in prestige of minority groups during this period was increased interest in one's racial/ethnic "roots." *Roots*, based on author Alex Haley's ancestors, beginning with his African progenitor Kunte Kinte's enslavement, both reflected this sentiment and stimulated popular interest in ethnic heritage. Nancy was already in her fifties when the *Roots* phenomenon took hold in the United States. However, she has a great hunger to remake connections with her Japanese ancestry. She did not have this same impulse prior to the 1970s, when being part Japanese in the United States had negative associations for her, primarily with wartime prejudices and fears. With the rise in ethnic pride during the 1960s and 1970s, however, the meaning of being something other than white became more positive for her and many other Americans. Yet, fundamentally, she identifies as Caucasian and American, and her interest in her Japanese heritage seems to be separate from her basic sense of identity. Interestingly, Nancy does not look Japanese, and her acquisition of Japanese culture and increasing identification with it is similar to the optional white ethnic identification described by Mary Waters (1990) among white European-heritage ethnics. This raises the question of whether some people of mixed race, particularly if they look white, can exert a similar optional ethnic identity. In Nancy's case, it seems that a mix of her getting older and societal developments combined to make her more inclined to explore her Japanese side.

Sam Cole, born in 1944 of mixed African American and Jewish ancestry, discussed wanting to learn more about his Jewish heritage—a relatively new phenomenon for him. Sam had some bitter memories of his early contacts with Judaism. Although his mother sent Sam and his brother to shul when they were boys to prepare for their bar mitzvah, their time there was short-lived.

> And so, here I'm going to shul with my brother, and we're learning the stuff we need to learn to be bar mitzvahed, and there were some new kids who came in one day, and we started hearing them calling us "schvartze, schvartze," and we didn't know what the hell a "schvartze" was. And it dawned on me and my brother that they were talking about us in a derogatory way. So I asked this one little girl what this meant. She said, "It means you're black." I said, "I'm not black." "Yes, you are. Look at your hair." I said, "Look at his hair." These Jewish kids had hair curlier than mine. "Well, look at your lips." "Well, look at their lips," you know. And so I found this really distasteful that now these kids were gonna try to tease us openly.... And my brother and I just walked out.

When Sam's Jewish mother heard how her children had been treated, she was furious and pulled the two boys out of shul. As a result, they were never formally trained in Judaism. The passage of time and changes within himself and the community around him have made Sam more eager to reconnect with Judaism in middle age. He said that he was thinking of formally studying Judaism with a rabbi. "I like the fact that the reform element of Judaism has seen fit to ordain women. That other men like Michael Lerner have sought to hold onto these traditions while giving comfort to people that were shunned in the orthodox community, homosexuals and stuff like this.... People have to find comfort with somebody." Thus, Sam's current feelings about Judaism combine how he has changed with age and how Judaism itself changed during the same period. This has been a dialectical process between his internal development and that of other Jews. Not only had he changed, but Judaism had changed.

Sometimes aging brings greater tolerance. Gus Pimental talked about the transformation in his attitudes. He admitted that for much of his early life, he hated white people because of his family's treatment by the white side of his family and by other whites who were against intermarriage. Yet, there were always contradictions in this stance; he never rejected his mother, and he had close friends who were white.

He said, "And so I could never reconcile that these people were okay, and somehow these other white people were all fucked up.... And so for a little bit I sort of lived a dishonesty. It wasn't a lie—it was a dishonesty in my own life, of rejecting white people." The older he gets, the less meaning race has for him. He sees people in more universal terms. For him, being of mixed race and being part of a multiracial family bring him closer to the ideal that we are "just one people."

> See to me, that's the beauty of mixed race. It's part of the beauty. We got all this stuff in us that brings in all kinds of things that people have, all people. And the older I get, the more I feel that. I look at my blond, blue-eyed grandchildren. I look at them and I think, man, look how beautiful they are. Period. No they're this and they're that.

Aging can bring a greater comfort with self, a greater centeredness. As one participant said, "Aging is about having a sense of where I am versus where they are." Having a better-developed sense of who they are paradoxically allowed participants more freedom to expand their definitions of self. Charles Daly, a mixed Japanese American born in 1949, put it succinctly when he said that middle age brought him "more reflectiveness and more to reflect back on." There is a sense that the biology of aging is less significant than the passage of time and the concomitant accumulation of experience, particularly for the middle-aged group. This was accompanied by a greater sense of self and clarity about identity. At the same time, there was less vigilance about defining the boundaries of self and more openness to exploration.

While those who were in their mid-sixties and older also described increased comfort with themselves as they aged, like most people of their age, they also associated aging with physical deterioration. There were some positives as well—primarily, being able to retire and having more time to do interesting things. But as Nancy Grant said, aging brings increasing health problems. When I asked her if she felt like the same person she did when she was younger, she replied, "No. I feel that it's the debilitating parts of aging that I don't like. We talk about this constantly, that if we could only make our—we all have acquired various ailments that we never had before, and are sick and tired of having so many medications and this and that." When I asked her about how she felt about who she is inside, aside from the physical changes, she said that she feels wiser due to the accumulation of experiences, particularly exposure to other cultures, which she acquired when she started traveling in her fifties. Like Nancy, most of the people her age and older have chronic health problems. Although many of them grew up in families in which herbal and folk remedies were used, the majority rely on Western medicine for their treatment.

This chapter has examined aging and mixed race identity in the context of the life course. The racial climate experienced by people during the formative years of adolescence and young adulthood seemed foundational to the perspectives on racial identity for the people I interviewed. Identity is constructed within systems that are vulnerable to shifts in power. The civil rights, Black Power, and other racial/ethnic power movements of the 1960s changed the meaning of blackness and color. This was reflected in changes in terminology rooted in fundamentally altered attitudes and beliefs about race. These changes affected people differently, based on their age when they experienced them.

With aging, the people I interviewed generally described a greater comfort with themselves and the full range of who they are. This can include exploring previously ignored parts of their backgrounds. There is a dialectical quality about their readiness to engage in these explorations; they have developed to the point at which this is possible, but so has society. In fact, it is impossible (and unproductive) to say which is primary, as people themselves are a part of society. As Sam said, "I changed. We all changed."

7

Can We Stand on Both Feet?

I have presented some of the ways older people experience and imagine mixed race identity differently based on factors like race, age, class, gender, and nationality. In this chapter, I shift focus to the commonalties, the themes that transcended differences, among the people I interviewed. Most of these common themes have already been touched upon in the quotations throughout this book. Here I want to make them explicit.

Discrimination

I use this word in the broadest sense, in relation to its root, "to discriminate." In its mildest sense, for the people in this book, it means to be noticed as racially different, to be discriminated from the backdrop of the normal. Within this context, people's experiences of discrimination ranged from being repeatedly noticed as racially "other" to being subjected to overt past practices that nowadays would be illegal, like school tracking and housing and employment discrimination. These experiences have taken place in the context of the legacy of the ideology of race and racial dictatorship, in which whiteness is considered normal and nonwhiteness is marked as "other." Within that context, all of the people I interviewed have been seen and treated as racially other. Race has entered into the lives of the mixed race people in this book as much as it has for people who don't consider themselves mixed, though in different ways. There are both differences from and similarities to the monoracial experience.

The people I talked with have experienced a sense of difference not only from whites but from other people of color. This came up primarily in relation to experienced dissonance between ascribed racial identity and cultural identity—in other words, between how they are viewed by others based on their physical characteristics and how they feel culturally. It is particularly an issue for the mixed African Americans I interviewed because of the omnipresence of an ascribed black identity for them, but it also arose for some of the mixed Asian Americans. The theme of authenticity is integral to this issue. What does it mean to be truly black? Or truly Asian American? Is it possible for a mixed race person to be considered fully a member of the community of the nonwhite parent? In addition to appearance, issues of culture, class, and language can mark the mixed race person as different from other African or Asian Americans.

There's also the question of how one deals with "hidden whiteness" when one is not clearly marked by appearance. Several of the participants I interviewed described situations in which the way other people of color talked about whites made them uncomfortable. It made them question their own integrity, how they should react, and whether they would still be accepted if they did react. For example, Fred Johnson, who was introduced to radical politics through black nationalism, eventually gravitated toward working with multiracial groups that were not organized strictly around race. It was hard to reconcile some of the antiwhite rhetoric coming out of the nationalist experience with the realities of having grown up in a family with a white parent. Fred described his difficulties: "I couldn't deal with the—at that time the Nation of Islam, and Mohammed Speaks, they would always caricature white people as pigs and monsters and all this stuff. And I didn't like that in general, and I knew I couldn't really take that on and still be a viable entity in the struggle. And at the same time, I felt very, like I was betraying my family, 'cause my grandmother's no pig, my mother's no pig." Fred also had to prove himself in black organizations. He was different not only because of the way he talked but also because he was always thinking beyond race as the primary motivating factor. He said, "Well, the story I heard was, guys saying, who's that proper-talkin' nigger anyway? 'Cause I didn't speak the right language. And I functioned more on principle than I did on race. And I didn't like certain ways in which some of the third world activists treated the white people. I didn't like it." Fred had to establish his authenticity because his talk was too "proper." He was also sensitive to antiwhite actions. As a mixed race African American, he risked losing credibility if he acknowledged his feelings and his white heritage. The polarization between blacks and whites has been particularly difficult for the mixed African Americans in this book. Fred expressed his opinion about people who want him to choose sides: "And I think their position is a no-growth position. It's a stagnating position. It's not gonna improve the quality of human life on this planet. I have opinions that, to the degree you cannot empathize with your enemy, who you define as your enemy, is to the degree when in power you will be [the same]." Fred's tendency to see both sides is mirrored by many of the people I interviewed.

Seeing Both Sides

It should be clear by now that the most consistent issue the mixed race people in this book faced in relationship to race was finding a place where they fit in and felt totally accepted. They don't have a natural racial community. While several of the people I interviewed did have strong ties to a community of color, their authenticity could still be challenged.

One way that mixed race people are challenged is around the issue of allegiance. When I asked people what they thought were the strengths of being mixed, the universal response was that, being mixed, they can see both sides in a conflict around race. Yet, paradoxically this can make them less accepted. Grace talked about this in terms of her African American friends noticing that she's comfortable with whites and how this makes her suspect. Either/or thinking is oppressive when you are both/and. Because of this, most of the people I talked with said they are most comfortable in multiracial settings and organizations that have a broader agenda than the issues of just one racial group.

The mixed race people in this book view as one of their greatest strengths the ability to feel comfortable with a broader range of people and situations than their monoracial counterparts. Several talked about how they blend in with a variety of different nationalities when traveling abroad, which they see as a definite advantage. They seem to have finely honed skills for absorbing the norms of other cultures quickly, possibly due to their many years of learning how to traverse difference. Many have found international experiences to be liberating and eye-opening in terms of exposure to the different ways of being seen and treated. Not looking like a "typical American" can be an advantage when abroad. It is impressive just how many of the people I interviewed have traveled or lived overseas for extensive periods. There may be some truth to the idealistic vision of mixed race people as the future "citizens of the world." Our first mixed race president provides an excellent example of this capability.

Yet, the two-sided nature of the fitting-in aspect of the mixed race experience requires further analysis. The lack of strong ties to a clearly defined community of reference can allow for more freedom to relate to a larger multinational, multiethnic community. However, the lack of a community of reference can also be profoundly unsettling. Particularly in the United States, where race is still such an important organizing factor in our lives, mixed race people can experience a great longing for a unified point of reference. Stuart Hall talks about the need for positionality in reference to ethnicity: "You have to position yourself somewhere in order to say anything at all. Thus, we cannot do without that sense of our own positioning that is connoted by the term ethnicity. And the relation that peoples of the world now have to their own past is, of course, part of the discovery of their own ethnicity" (1991, 18). What does it mean not to have an ethnicity, to lack "positionality?" For one thing, it can get pretty lonely. As Fred Johnson said, "There is a loneliness, and the loneliness is around not connecting on that issue with anybody else." Existentially, several of the mixed race people in this book are simultaneously at home everywhere and nowhere. People may deal with this in a variety of ways, without feeling they are in contradiction. For example, they may embrace a black identity, while simultaneously acknowledging it as a multiracial identity, while also seeking connection with the nonblack aspects of their background. Others may consciously study previously neglected aspects of their heritages, like Nancy, who at the age of seventy-six was actively studying Japanese language, film, and art, as well as preparing to take a trip to Japan. In this sense, mixed race people are not that different from those who define themselves as monoracial, who may also be actively engaged in constructing and reconstructing the meaning of ethnic identity for themselves. There is an element of racial or ethnic identity in the contemporary period that is, of necessity, constructed. Again, I found Hall's discussion of the character of ethnicity very relevant:

> So the relationship of the kind of ethnicity I'm talking about to the past is not a simple, essential one—it is a constructed one. It is constructed in history, it is constructed politically in part. It is part of narrative. We tell ourselves the stories of the parts of our roots in order to come into contact, creatively, with it. So this new kind of ethnicity—the emergent ethnicities—has a relationship to the past, but it is a relationship that is partly through memory, partly through narrative, one that has to be recovered. It is an act of cultural recovery. (1991, 19)

Racial and ethnic identity will continue to have meaning for mixed race people. But will mixed race become an "emergent ethnicity" in its own right? And what will it mean for the fast-emerging generation of youth of multiple mixed ancestries, who make the binary ancestries of the people in this book seem simple by comparison?

Can We Stand on Both Feet?

This book began with a quote from Fred Johnson about the liberatory effect of "standing on both feet," of experiencing himself as a mixed race person rather than always hopping from one foot to the other. He and growing numbers of younger mixed race people are exercising agency in pro-actively defining their identities as a kind of third space that is different from, but inclusive of, both parent identities. There is a great need for groups in which mixed race people can feel authenticated and give support to each other. A sign of this has been the rapid growth of mixed race organizations. These are all progressive developments in undoing the power of racial essentialisms and the ideology of race. Yet, while there is a great yearning among younger mixed race people for an actual mixed race community to call their own, how likely is this to develop?

Some have argued that if there is no such thing as race, how can mixed race people who oppose the tyranny of racial categories create another category that, by its nature, assumes the existence of race? There is a fundamental problem of logic in the idea of mixed race within the existing categories. And race does not exist as an objective entity outside those categories. In a sense, we are still prisoners of the prevailing discourses of race. State-created racial categories still influence our perceptions of available alternatives, even as we oppose them.

There is also the question of whether mixed race can exist as a collective identity. There was no singular, discrete "mixed race identity" for the people I interviewed. What ties would bind a collective mixed race identity? As Michael Thornton points out, "In fact, what seems to bind multiracial people is not race or culture, but living with an ambiguous status, an experience similar to that of all people of color. Facing a different set of dilemmas does not make one an ethnic or racial group, or signify a culture. As a group, multiracials are too diverse to categorize" (1992, 324). I disagree with Thornton that the ambiguous status of mixed race people is common to all people of color. It is precisely because multiracials are outside the boundaries of racial definitions that they suffer from ambiguity. However, he rightly questions whether the common experience of ambiguity is sufficient as a basis for a collective identity. Certainly new collective ethnicities have been consciously created, such as "Asian American" (Espiritu 1992; Lott 1997). But Asian Americans shared the common experience of being identified by their Asian "race," which transcended national boundaries and gave them a collective basis upon which to build this coalition identity. And more recent Asian immigrants may identify less as Asian American and more with their nationality of origin. It remains to be seen whether the shared experience of racial ambiguity and alienation will be enough to forge a new collective identity for people of mixed race. Certainly, the possibility of such a collective formation is made more difficult by the racial rules that have been applied to different groups. We have seen the differences in the way the older mixed African and Asian Americans in this book view their identities. State-imposed definitions have had many generations to make themselves real to those to whom they have applied. People have developed cultural identities incorporating those definitions. It is also interesting that as mixed race organizations have evolved, some have tended to be dominated by one nonwhite racial ancestry, such as Hapa Issues Forum, which focused primarily on mixed Asian Americans.

I think it unlikely that a sense of community for mixed race people can be firmly established on racial identity alone. I believe that the future of mixed race people finding community is tied to the future of movements that challenge the fundamental assumptions of a system based on exploitation that justifies its practices through an ideology of racial inequality. The construct of race, which so plagues mixed race people, will not end until the ideology of race and the inequality it justifies end. In the meantime, mixed race people will continue to search for and find community in a variety of ways: through identification with their backgrounds, through mixed race groups, and in all the other places where nonmixed people find community—in activities and organizations based on common interests and goals and not solely on racial identity.

I embarked on this endeavor focused on questions related to the construction of identity for older mixed race people, how it varies based on whether the parent of color was of African or Asian ancestry, and how identity intersects with aging for this group. Finding that identity was not a fixed entity for the people I interviewed, I organized what people said about it into five dimensions of mixed race identity. Although some of these dimensions were situational, some of the most powerful, like ascribed racial identity, were not, particularly for mixed African Americans. The mixed African Americans I interviewed expressed less choice in identification than the mixed Asian Americans. In terms of the interaction of aging with mixed race identity, the most powerful effect seems to be the intersection of the life course with history. People's age when they experienced the gains made by minority groups and the rise in ethnic identity movements in the 1960s was particularly important. Gender, class, and family were also significant elements in the construction of identity.

The structural inequality that evolved from the racial dictatorship (Omi and Winant 1994) forms the background for the construction of identity for the people in this book. Representations of race have been influenced by fluctuations in power; therefore, there have been historical changes in them (Hall 1997). They changed fundamentally in the 1960s when social movements of resistance forced a change in the balance of power. Mixed race people, like everyone else, absorb these discourses and representations and are influenced by them in their interpretations of race and assignment of identity to themselves and others.

Identity itself is a social construction, and racial identity is always negotiated in relationship to difference (Hall 1997). Thus, for mixed race people, the situational character of the construction of identity is particularly apparent, since they are the embodiment of difference. Identity and identification are produced at the level of day-to-day interaction, where people create their sense of identity through their exchanges with each other (Mead [1929] 1993) and their collective perceptions of where they stand racially (Lyman 1988).

However, the spaces available for identity construction have been defined by the degree of institutional power and control over rules for racial classification. The rigidity of the lines of demarcation around people of African descent is the prime example of this. Although the terms may have changed, mixed people of African ancestry in the United States are still overwhelmingly identified by others on the basis of that ancestry alone. This is reinforced by both blacks and whites, and there are real penalties for identifying as anything other than black. As a result, unlike many of the mixed Asian Americans, who are identified in a variety of ways by others, there is consistency between the ways mixed African Americans identify themselves *to* others and how they are identified *by* others.

Power is everywhere in this story. Power, or the lack of it, is the reason members of the older generation in my study tend to identify more as American or Caucasian. When they were coming of age, there was no sustained challenge to the racial dictatorship. There was certainly resistance but nothing comparable to the social movements that produced the structural changes of the 1960s, with their attendant changes in representations of what it meant not to be white. Assimilation was valued in their time, when the more white one was, the better one's chances were. Those representations did not change in a vacuum. They changed because of real shifts in power—concessions made because of the strength of social movements, most notably the civil rights movement and subsequent ethnic power movements that fundamentally challenged this country to change the way its citizens see color. These concessions had the potential to make being a person of color an advantage for the first time in employment and education. During this period, members of social movements based on ethnic identity also tried to achieve solidarity with each other as "third world people" or as "people of color." The term *third world* explicitly acknowledged the connection between communities of color in the United States and their international counterparts, many of which were engaged in anticolonial struggles for national liberation during the same period. The age cohort differences reflect the difference between coming of age when white supremacy was virtually uncontested, as opposed to during a time when people of color were fighting real battles and winning some of them, resulting in transfers of power.

Representations of gender and class interact with and shape race and vice versa. Since people of color, particularly blacks, have been at the bottom of the racial hierarchy, it makes sense that class in particular should be intertwined with race. The people in this book absorbed popular representations of race like anyone else. The remarks they make about class also indicate the degree to which race is not strictly about color. There is a popular saying that "money whitens." People in my study perceive themselves and others to be more or less "colored" or "of color" based on behavioral traits that are associated with class status.

This is also true of gender. The "gendering of ethnicity" produced by white ideology, referred to by Yen Le Espiritu (1997), plays itself out in two ways for the people I interviewed. One is in the different ways that mixed race identity is mediated by gender for the mixed African American men and women. The other is the ways that images of race itself are gendered, so that, for example, images associated with Asian identity were feminized by some participants, although this has not always been the case. Such representations of race are historically mediated and may change with shifting ideologies (Hall 1997).

Power is crucial to the meaning of mixed race in other nations too. Imperialism and colonialism in China and the Philippines shaped the meaning of being mixed there. In prerevolutionary China, Eurasians were treated differently by the Europeans because they were part Chinese. They were better accepted by the Chinese because they were part European. This illustrates how the association of white superiority and Western supremacy is a global project. These mixed Asians formed a distinct stratum as Eurasians. Class played a role in how the mixed person was treated in other countries as well. In the Philippines, at the street level, Louise Soriano was confronted by a taunt implying that her mother was a prostitute, but in the schools, as a middle-class mestiza, she was treated better than the other children.

Who has power and who doesn't in the various contexts in which mixed people find themselves heavily influences their circumstances and, in turn, how they identify. Power is dynamic and can shift, and meanings can change with these shifts. For example, some younger mixed race women I've interviewed in another study report feeling more stigma associated with their whiteness than with their color. This may be due to changes in the relative values of color and whiteness in the post–civil rights era. Yet, this position suffers from the same root of essentialist thinking as its opposite. An ideology based on affirming the positiveness of color, which was originally progressive in its link to radical social movements at home and abroad, can become co-opted when color in and of itself becomes "good" and white is stigmatized. Replacing one essentialized stereotype with its opposite is not truly liberatory. A truly counterhegemonic strategy would radically challenge the ideology of race and its essentialist division of human beings into races. Opposing whites and whiteness purely on a racial basis without critiquing the underlying structure that perpetuates inequality is only a partial strategy that perpetuates the belief in the reality of race, mirroring white supremacy.

Future Possibilities

What does the future hold for the rapidly growing population of mixed race people? We have seen how the era of progress in civil rights and the rise in identity politics in the 1960s influenced people who are now elderly or fast approaching that status. Since that period there has been a sharp increase in interracial marriage. However, the rates of out-marriage and the particular mixes of the children of those marriages are far from uniform. Relatively low rates of African American out-marriage in comparison with other groups of color (Passel, Wang, and Taylor 2010) lead some to envision a society that is no longer racially defined by the white/nonwhite dichotomy but by black and nonblack, "the beige and the black" (Lind 1998). Others see the emergence of a trilevel racial stratification system (Bonilla-Silva 2004). These projections share a belief that African Americans will continue to remain at the bottom of the racial hierarchy, "left out of the melting pot once again" (Lind 1998).

Anticolonial movements abroad, domestic ethnic power movements, and civil rights legislation, including affirmative action, all challenged the racial balance of power and gave more voice to sentiments of resistance in the 1960s and 1970s. Yet, there is an instability to the gains minority groups have made. Widening inequality is reflected in the growth of disparities between the health of African Americans and others. At the same time, we have a mixed race president of African ancestry, and we are told this means we are in a "postracial" era.

Younger cohorts of mixed race people are facing a set of circumstances and relations of power that may be the most complex ever. People of mixed race ancestry have become far more visible in the last decade. Important national developments, such as the change in the 2000 U.S. census allowing people to identify with more than one racial category, have provided new legitimacy and visibility to the multiracial population. Prominent people of acknowledged mixed ancestry can be found in entertainment, sports, and politics. In 2008 we elected our first mixed race president, though he is still overwhelmingly described as black. People of ambiguous racial appearance are much more apparent in the highly influential worlds of advertising and the media, which both reflect and project images of desirable, acceptable human beings to the public. A young mixed race person stands a good chance of seeing him- or herself somewhere in film, TV, or advertising. In fact, we are witnessing the commodification of mixed race. These days, people of racially ambiguous appearance are a hot item, and my cynicism tells me it's because advertisers recognize the value of reaching "two or more for the price of one" racial groups.

Does this mean things will be easier for new generations of mixed race people? There are hopeful signs; yet, the belief that race is real and that the races are distinct runs deep. As long as the majority of America still believes in the reality of race and the ideology of race remains unexamined, external validation of all that they are will be hard to come by for multiracial people. It disturbs me that in more recent interviews with young mixed race women, I have found that many endure some of the same struggles for legitimacy and coherence that their older counterparts did. Though much has changed, too much has not. We are not yet in a "postracial" America. But perhaps the increasing visibility of people of mixed race and increased understanding of their experiences will help deconstruct the ideology of race. Being a racial outsider provides for the possibility of a heightened awareness of the inconsistencies and absurdities of a racialized epistemology that most of the population takes for granted. The stories of mixed race people demonstrate the everyday existential dilemmas that result from being an outsider in a society in which race is one of the most powerful identifiers. They tell of the particular pain that an extremely racialized system can produce for the person for whom there is no easy place of belonging. Personal experience can be a point of entry for the larger project of undermining the power of race. It will be important to track how changing representations of race and mixed race will influence the meaning people give to their racial identities as new cohorts are born and age. Why study people of mixed race? Because it brings us a step closer to dismantling our belief system about race and thus strikes a blow against the behavior associated with that belief, which is racism. The stories of the people in this book provide a profoundly important foundation for that project.

It is clear from the stories people shared with me that movements for justice and equality can have a profound impact on patterns of intermarriage and the meaning of being a person of color, thus mixed race. It is also apparent that there will be no decline in the significance of race until we undo the ideology of race and address inequality, particularly for African Americans. Mixed race people are most vulnerable to the continuing significance of race; it can pull them apart, make them deny parts of themselves, and impose a sense of dissonance upon their selfhood. Yet, their very existence is cause for hope as a sign of the continuing erosion of the ideology of race. As a society, we can learn much from their unique vantage point on racial differences. Mixed race people will continue to resist the ideology of race by pointing out its absurdities. They need to share their stories with others to learn that they are not alone. Being supported offers a base for resistance. And finally, they need to fight to make our nation truly a place where each of us, regardless of race, can "stand on both feet."

Appendix A

Dimensions of Identity

Name	Year Born	Heritage[1]	Cultural ID	Ascribed ID	Racial ID (to Others)	Racial Self-ID
Janet	1902	Chinese/Danish	Western	Eurasian	Eurasian	Eurasian
Jane	1916	German American/Japanese	American	Japanese	Half Japanese/half American	American Japanese
Nancy	1921	Canadian/Japanese	Caucasian, American	White, Japanese during WWII	Other, Eurasian	Caucasian, American
Taylor	1925	Russian/Filipino	American	Uncertain	Half Russian/half Filipino	American
Caroline	1927	French/Chinese	Eurasian	Eurasian, not-white	Asian	Eurasian
Gretchen	1931	German American/Japanese	American Japanese	Japanese, mixed	American Japanese	Both, half Japanese, half German, American
Louise	1931	White/Filipino	Filipino, Asian	Asian, Filipino, Mexican, Indian, mestizo	Asian	Filipino, Asian
Alicia	1936	Chinese/Portuguese/Filipino	Portuguese, Eurasian	Asian, Chinese, Hawaiian, Filipino, Hispanic	Other, Eurasian, everything that applies	Mixed, Eurasian
Gus	1939	White/Filipino	Filipino American	Mestizo, Chicano, Italian	Filipino, Spanish, Scottish	Filipino American, mestizo
Todd	1939	Jewish/Japanese	American, whatever culture he's around	Japanese in WWII, Indian, Latino	Eurasian	Both, neither
Mary	1944	White/Filipino	Primarily white	Brown, not-white	Filipino American	Mixed, unique, Filipino
Joseph	1946	Japanese American/Irish American	American	Asian, Mexican, Filipino, Indian	Other	Rebel, Asian, brown, Irish
Charles	1948	Japanese American/Irish American	White, Japanese	Asian, Hispanic, Filipino, third world	Parents' ethnicity, Asian, Japanese	Third world, nonwhite, American
Helen	1931	Black[2]/white	Colored	Colored	Colored	Colored
Brian	1939	White/black	Primarily white	Black	Black, person of color	Person of color, black
Fred	1941	White/black	Fluid	Black	Negro, black, mixed, other	Person of color, black, mixed
Sam	1944	Jewish/black	Black and Jewish	Black	Black	Black, "wannabe black Jew," biracial
Larry	1946	Irish American/black	White, "not either"	Black	Black	"Something else," minority person, third world
Grace	1948	White/black	White and black	Black, other	Black	Black
Kim	1951	Jewish/black	Black and Jewish	Black, Latin, Indian	Black	Black who's also a Hungarian Jew and Native American

1. Mother's ancestry is listed first.

2. Parent self-defined as black. Most of the parents who identified as black also had white and Native American ancestry.

References

Almaguer, T. 1994. *Racial fault lines: The historical origins of white supremacy in California.* Berkeley: University of California Press.

Anthias, F., and N. Yuval-Davis. 1992. *Racialized boundaries.* London and New York: Routledge.

Becker, G. 1997. *Disrupted lives.* Berkeley: University of California Press.

Berger, M. T., and K. Guidroz. 2010. *The intersectional approach.* Chapel Hill: University of North Carolina Press.

Bonilla-Silva, E. 2003. *Racism without racists: Color-blind racism and the persistence of racial inequality in the United States.* Lanham, MD: Rowman & Littlefield.

————. 2004. From biracial to tri-racial: The emergence of a new racial stratification system in the United States. In *Skin/deep: How race and complexion matter in the "color-blind" era,* edited by C. Herring, V. M. Keith, and H. D. Horton, 224–239. Urbana and Chicago: University of Illinois Press.

Bourdieu, P. 1977. *Outline of a theory of practice.* Cambridge: Cambridge University Press.

Bourdieu, P., and L. J. D. Wacquant. 1992. *An invitation to reflexive sociology.* Chicago: University of Chicago Press.

Bratter, J., and H. E. Heard. 2009. Mother's, father's or both? Parental gender and parent-child interactions in the racial classification of adolescents. *Sociological Forum* 24, no. 3: 658–688.

Brunsma, D. L. 2005. Interracial families and the racial identification of mixed-race children: Evidence from the early childhood longitudinal study. *Social Forces* 84, no. 20: 1131–1157.

Chan, S. 1991. *Asian Americans: An interpretive history.* Boston: Twayne Publishers.

Cheng, S., and K. J. Lively. 2009. Multiracial self-identification and adolescent outcomes: A social psychological approach to the marginal man theory. *Social Forces* 88, no. 1: 61–98.

Chesneaux, J., M. Bastid, and M. C. Bergere. 1976. *China: From the Opium Wars to the 1911 revolution.* New York: Pantheon Books.

Chin, G. 2002. Preserving racial identity: Population patterns and the application of anti-miscegenation statutes to Asian Americans, 1910–1950. *Berkeley Asian Law Journal* 9: 1–40.

Conley, D. 1999. *Being black, living in the red: Race, wealth, and social policy in America.* Berkeley: University of California Press.

Cooley, C. H. [1902] 1993. The looking-glass self. In *Social theory: The multicultural and classic readings,* edited by C. Lemert, 204–205. Boulder, CO: Westview Press.

Corbett, C. 2010. *The poker bride: The first Chinese in the West.* New York: Atlantic Monthly Press.

Crenshaw, K. W. 1995. Mapping the margins: Intersectionality, identity politics, and violence against women of color. In *Critical race theory,* edited by K. Crenshaw, N. Gotanda, G. Peller, and K. Thomas, 357–383. New York: The New Press.

Cross, J. 2006. *Secret daughter: A mixed-race daughter and the mother who gave her away.* New York: Viking.

Cross, W. E., Jr. 1971. Negro-to-black conversion experience. *Black World* 20: 13–27.

Davis, F. J. 1991. *Who is black?* University Park: University of Pennsylvania Press.

Dien, D. S. 2000. The evolving nature of self-identity across four levels of history. *Human Development* 43: 1–18.

Dominguez, V. R. 1994. *White by definition.* New Brunswick, NJ: Rutgers University Press.

Dressler, W. 1991. Social class, skin color, and arterial blood pressure in two societies. *Ethnicity and Disease* 1: 60–77.

Elder, G. 1974. *Children of the Great Depression.* Chicago: University of Chicago Press.

———. 1995. The life course paradigm: Social change and individual development. In *Examining lives in context: Perspectives on the ecology of human development,* edited by P. Moen, G. H. Elder, and K. Luscher, 101–130. Washington, DC: American Psychological Association.

———. 1998. The life course as developmental theory. *Child Development* 69, no. 1: 1–12.

Erikson, E. 1950. *Childhood and society.* New York: Norton.

Espiritu, Y. L. 1992. *Asian American panethnicity.* Philadelphia: Temple University Press.

———. 1997. *Asian American women and men.* Thousand Oaks, CA: Sage.

Fanon, F. 1967. *Black skin, white masks.* New York: Grove Weidenfield.

Feagin, J. 2006. *Systemic racism: A theory of oppression.* New York: Routledge.

Feagin, J., and E. O'Brien. 2003. *White men on race.* Boston: Beacon.

Featherstone, M., and M. Hepworth. 1991. The mask of ageing and the postmodern life course. In *The body: Social processes and cultural theory,* edited by M. Featherstone, M. Hepworth, and B. S. Turner, 371–389. London: Sage.

Ferber, A. 1998. *White man falling: Race, gender, and white supremacy.* Lanham, MD: Rowman & Littlefield.

Frank, G. 1979. Finding the common denominator: A phenomenological critique of life history method. *Ethos* 7: 68–94.

Frankenberg, R. 1993. *White women, race matters: The social construction of whiteness.* Minneapolis: University of Minnesota Press.

Franklin, J. H., and A. A. Moss. 1994. *From slavery to freedom: A history of African Americans.* 7th ed. New York: McGraw-Hill, Inc.

Fredrickson, G. 1981. *White supremacy: A comparative study of American and South African history.* New York: Oxford University Press.

Funderburg, L. 1994. *Black, white, other.* New York: William Morrow.

Gee, J. P. 1992. *The social mind: Language, ideology, and social practice.* New York: Bergin & Garvey.

Gilman, S. 1985. *Difference and pathology.* Ithaca, NY: Cornell University Press.

Gleason, P. [1983] 1996. Identifying identity: A semantic history. In *Theories of ethnicity: A classical reader,* edited by W. Sollors, 460–487. New York: New York University Press.

Glenn, E. N. 2002. *Unequal freedom: How race and gender shaped American citizenship and labor.* Cambridge, MA: Harvard University Press.

Goffman, I. 1959. *The presentation of self in everyday life.* New York: Anchor Books Doubleday.

———. 1963. *Stigma: Notes on the management of a spoiled identity.* Englewood Cliffs, NJ: Prentice Hall.

Gross, A. J. 2003. Litigating whiteness: Trials of racial determination in the nineteenth-century South. In *Mixed race America and the law,* edited by K. R. Johnson, 111–117. New York: New York University Press.

Gubrium, J. F., and J. A. Holstein. 2003. *Ways of aging.* Malden, MA: Blackwell Publishing.

Hall, S. 1991. Ethnicity: Identity and difference. *Radical America* 23, no. 4: 9–19.

———. 1997. The work of representation. In *Representation: Cultural representations and signifying practices,* edited by S. Hall, 13–74. Thousand Oaks, CA: Sage.

Han Suyin. [1966] 1985. *A mortal flower.* London: Triad Panther.

Haney Lopez, I. 1996. *White by law: The legal construction of race.* New York: New York University Press.

Harris, D. R., and J. J. Sim. 2002. Who is multiracial? Assessing the complexity of lived race. *American Sociological Review* 67, no. 4: 614–627.

Hearth, A. H., S. L. Delany, and A. E. Delany. 1993. *Having our say*. New York: Dell.

Herman, M. 2004. Forced to choose: Some determinants of racial identification in multiracial adolescents. *Child Development* 75, no. 3: 730–748.

Herring, C., V. M. Keith, and H. D. Horton, eds. 2004. *Skin/deep: How race and complexion matter in the "color-blind" era*. Urbana and Chicago: University of Illinois Press.

Hickman, C. B. 2003. The devil and the "one-drop" rule. In *Mixed race America and the law*, edited by K. R. Johnson, 104–110. New York: New York University Press.

Higginbotham, L., and B. K. Kopytoff. 2003. Racial purity and interracial sex in the law of colonial and antebellum Virginia. In *Mixed race America and the law*, edited by K. R. Johnson, 13–27. New York: New York University Press.

Hill Collins, P. 2001. *Black feminist thought*. New York: Routledge.

———. 2004. *Black sexual politics*. New York and London: Routledge.

Hing, B. O. 1993. *Making and remaking Asian America through immigration policy, 1850–1990*. Stanford, CA: Stanford University Press.

Hitlin, S., J. S. Brown, and G. H. Elder. 2006. Racial self-categorization in adolescence: Multiracial development and social pathways. *Child Development* 77, no. 5: 1298–1308.

Holstein, J. A., and J. F. Gubrium. 2000a. *Constructing the life course*. Dix Hills, NY: General Hall.

———. 2000b. *The self we live by: Narrative identity in a postmodern world*. New York: Oxford University Press.

Jackson, J. S., L. M. Chatters, and R. J. Taylor. 1993. Status and functioning of future cohorts of African-American elderly. In *Aging in black America*, edited by J. S. Jackson, L. M. Chatters, and R. J. Taylor, 301–316. Newbury Park, CA: Sage.

Jenkins, R. 1992. *Pierre Bourdieu*. London: Routledge.

Johnson, M. S. 1993. *The second gold rush: Oakland and the East Bay in World War II*. Berkeley: University of California Press.

Kaufman, S. R. 1986. *The ageless self: Sources of meaning in late life*. Madison: University of Wisconsin Press.

Khanna, N. 2004. The role of reflected appraisals in racial identity: The case of multiracial Asians. *Social Psychology Quarterly* 67, no. 2: 115–131.

Kich, G. K. 1992. The developmental process of asserting a biracial, bicultural identity. In *Racially mixed people in America*, edited by M. P. P. Root, 304–317. Newbury Park, CA: Sage.

King, R. C., and K. M. DaCosta. 1996. Changing face, changing race: The remaking of race in the Japanese American and African American communities. In *The multiracial experience: Racial borders as the new frontier,* edited by M. P. P. Root, 227–244. Thousand Oaks, CA: Sage.

Lind, M. 1998. The beige and the black. *New York Times Magazine,* August 10, 1998.

Loewen, J. W. 1988. *The Mississippi Chinese: Between black and white.* 2nd ed. Project Heights, IL: Waveland Press, Inc.

Lott, J. T. 1997. *Asian Americans: From racial category to multiple identities.* Walnut Creek, CA: Altamira Press.

Luborsky, M. 1993. The romance with personal meaning in gerontology: Cultural aspects of life themes. *The Gerontologist* 33: 445–452.

Luborsky, M., and R. L. Rubinstein. 1987. Ethnicity and lifetimes: Self-concepts and situational contexts of ethnic identity in late life. In *Ethnic dimensions of aging,* edited by Donald E. Gelfand and Charles M. Barresi, 35–50. New York: Springer.

Lyman, S. 1988. *Social order and the public philosophy: An analysis and interpretation of the work of Herbert Blumer.* Fayetteville: University of Arkansas Press.

Mannheim, K. [1928] 1997. The problem of generations. In *Studying aging and social change: Conceptual and methodological issues,* edited by M. Hardy, 22–65. Thousand Oaks, CA: Sage.

Mead, G. H. [1929] 1993. The self, the I, and the me. In *Social theory: The multicultural and classic readings,* edited by C. Lemert, 243–247. Boulder, CO: Westview Press.

Mercer, K. 1994. Reading racial fetishism. In *Welcome to the jungle,* edited by K. Mercer, 171–220. London: Routledge.

Meyer, J. 1988. Levels of analysis: The life course as a cultural construction. In *Social structures and human lives,* edited by M. White, 49–62. Beverly Hills, CA: Sage.

Meyerhoff, B. 1978. *Number our days.* New York: Simon & Schuster.

Mura, D. 1996. *Where the body meets memory: An odyssey of race, sexuality and identity.* New York: Anchor.

Odo, F. 2002. *The Columbia documentary history of the Asian American experience.* New York: Columbia University Press.

Okihiro, G. 2001. *The Columbia guide to Asian American history.* New York: Columbia University Press.

Omi, M., and H. Winant. 1994. *Racial formation in the United States.* New York: Routledge.

Pascoe, P. 1996. Miscegenation law, court cases, and ideologies of "race" in twentieth-century America. *Journal of American History* (June): 44–69.

Passel, J. S., W. Wang, and P. Taylor. 2010. Marrying out: One-in-seven new

U.S. marriages is interracial or interethnic. Pew Research Center. June 4. www.pewresearch.org/pubs/1616/american-marriage-interracial -interethnic.

Provine, W. B. 1986. Geneticists and race. *American Zoology* 26: 857–887.

Rockquemore, K. A. 2002. Negotiating the color line: The gendered process of racial identity construction among black/white biracial women. *Gender & Society* 16, no. 4: 485–503.

Rockquemore, K. A., and D. L. Brunsma. 2002. Socially embedded identities: Theories, typologies, and processes of racial identity among black/white biracials. *Sociological Quarterly* 43, no. 3: 335–356.

Rockquemore, K. A., D. L. Brunsma, and D. J. Delgado. 2009. Race to theory or retheorizing race: Understanding the struggle to build a multiracial identity theory. *Journal of Social Issues* 65, no. 1: 13–34.

Rockquemore, K. A., T. Lasyloffy, and J. Noveske. 2006. It all starts at home: Racial socialization in multiracial families. In *Mixed messages: Multiracial identities in the "color-blind" era*, edited by D. L. Brunsma, 203–216. Boulder, CO: Lynne Rienner.

Root, M. P. P. 2001. *Love's revolution: Interracial marriages*. Philadelphia: Temple University Press.

Rosenthal, G. 1993. Reconstruction of life stories: Principles of selection in generating stories for narrative biographical interviews. In *The narrative study of lives*, edited by R. Josselson and A. Lieblich, 59–91. Newbury Park, CA: Sage.

Schiebinger, L. 1993. *Nature's body*. Boston: Beacon Press.

Shinagawa, L., and M. Jang. 1998. *Atlas of American diversity*. Walnut Creek, CA: Altamira Press.

Smith, R. J., and M. C. Thornton. 1993. Identity and consciousness: Group solidarity. In *Aging in black America*, edited by J. S. Jackson, L. M. Chatters, and R. J. Taylor, 203–216. Newbury Park, CA: Sage.

Spencer, R. 2006. *Challenging multiracial identity*. Boulder, CO: Lynne Rienner.

Spickard, P. R. 1989. *Mixed blood: Intermarriage and ethnic identity in twentieth-century America*. Madison: University of Wisconsin Press.

Steinberg, S. 1981. *The ethnic myth*. New York: Atheneum.

Stoller, W. P., and R. C. Gibson. 2000. *Worlds of difference: Inequality in the aging experience*. 3rd ed. Thousand Oaks, CA: Pine Forge Press.

Sweet, E., T. W. McDade, C. I. Kief, and K. Liu. 2007. Relationships between skin color, income, and blood pressure among African Americans in the CARDIA study. *American Journal of Public Health* 97, no. 12: 2253–2259.

Takaki, R. 1989. *Strangers from a different shore*. Boston: Little, Brown and Company.

Tashiro, C. J. 2002. Considering the significance of ancestry through the prism of mixed-race identity. *Advances in Nursing Science* 25, no. 2: 1–21.

————. 2005. Health disparities in the context of mixed race: Challenging the ideology of race. *Advances in Nursing Science* 28, no. 3: 203–211.

Thornton, M. 1992. Is multiracial status unique? The personal and social experience. In *Racially mixed people in America,* edited by M. P. P. Root. Newbury Park, CA: Sage.

————. 1996. Hidden agendas, identity theories, and multiracial people. In *The multiracial experience: Racial borders as the new frontier,* edited by M. P. P. Root, 101–120. Thousand Oaks, CA: Sage.

U.S. Census Bureau. 2011. Profile of general population and housing characteristics: 2010 demographic profile data. American FactFinder. http://factfinder2.census.gov/faces/tableservices/jsf/pages/productview.xhtml?pid=DEC_10_DP_DPDP1&prodType=table.

Wallace, K. 2001. *Relative/outsider: The art and politics of identity among mixed heritage students.* Westport, CT: Ablex Publishing.

Waters, M. 1990. *Ethnic options: Choosing identities in America.* Berkeley: University of California Press.

Widdershoven, G. A. A. 1993. The story of life: Hermeneutic perspectives on the relationship between narrative and life history. In *The narrative study of lives,* edited by R. Josselson and A. Lieblich, 1–20. Newbury Park, CA: Sage.

Williams, G. H. 1996. *Life on the color line.* New York: Penguin.

Williamson, J. 1995. *New people: Miscegenation and mulattoes in the United States.* Baton Rouge: Louisiana State University Press.

Winant, H. 1994. *Racial conditions.* Minneapolis: University of Minnesota Press.

Yancey, G., and R. Lewis Jr. 2009. *Interracial families: Current concepts and controversies.* New York: Routledge.

Zack, N. 1995. *American mixed race: Constructing microdiversity.* Lanham, MD: Rowman & Littlefield.

Index

About the Author

Cathy J. Tashiro is Emeritus faculty in the Nursing Program at the University of Washington, Tacoma. She has a unique background as a health care provider and sociologist. She has published articles and book chapters on mixed race identity, mixed race and health disparities, and the meaning of race in health care and research. Prior to obtaining her PhD in Sociology at the University of California, San Francisco, Cathy worked in women's health and in many community-based settings with diverse populations as a nurse, nurse practitioner, and consultant.